News of the Universe

The seat of the soul is where the inner world
and the outer world meet. Where they overlap,
it is in every point of the overlap.

Novalis
translated by Charles E. Passage

NEWS OF THE UNIVERSE poems
of twofold consciousness

chosen and introduced by ROBERT BLY

It is suspect
when the author, shunning
fine existing translations,
chooses to translate for
himself so that he can
make his point
thereby (not, perhaps,
the author's point.)

SIERRA CLUB BOOKS   SAN FRANCISCO

The Sierra Club, founded in 1892 by John Muir, has devoted itself to
the study and protection of the earth's scenic and ecological resources—
mountains, wetlands, woodlands, wild shores and rivers, deserts and plains.
The publishing program of the Sierra Club offers books to the public as a
nonprofit educational service in the hope that they may enlarge the public's
understanding of the Club's basic concerns. The point of view expressed
in each book, however, does not necessarily represent that of the Club. The
Sierra Club has some sixty chapters coast to coast, in Canada, Hawaii, and
Alaska. For information about how you may participate in its programs to
preserve wilderness and the quality of life, please address inquiries to
Sierra Club, 730 Polk Street, San Francisco, CA 94109.

Library of Congress Cataloging in Publication Data
Main entry under title:
News of the universe.
    Includes index.
    I. Poetry—Collections.   I. Bly, Robert.
PN6101.N4   808.81'9'35   79-12812
ISBN 0-87156-368-1

Designed by James Robertson and Diana Fairbanks,
The Yolla Bolly Press, Covelo, California.
Typeset in Kennerly by Mackenzie-Harris Corp.
Cover photograph by John Hendrickson.

Printed in the United States of America on acid-free paper containing a
minimum of 50% recovered waste paper, of which at least 10% of the fiber
content is post-consumer waste

10 9 8 7 6 5 4 3 2 1

for Kenneth Rexroth

"One day the master imagined
a new blossoming."

Contents

vii

viii

Preface to the New Edition

THE Sierra Club has kept *News of the Universe* in print since 1980, and I am very pleased that they are re-issuing it now with a new cover and a new launching. The subject of the book is the contrast in our culture between the universe and the practical human mind. Something in the human mind is very greedy and will not admit that "Nature" contains anything more wonderful than human intellect.

As soon as we wake out of womb-sleep, we rise, one could say, into irritable consciousness, then to childhood clarity, then to confused adolescence, and we finally arrive at the practical intellect, which seems to be our goal. It is literal, and enables us to use, scientifically, all the forces of the universe.

The United States, during World War II, found that by dint of the practical intellect it could produce a hundred tanks a day and twenty B-52s; by doing so, the U.S. established itself as a world power. Something new was born, but if you don't invite Nature to your baptism, the baby will be cursed.

Saints say that if we could only take one step beyond the practical intellect—to the spiritual intellect—we could honor Nature because we then would realize that the whole universe is shot through with some sort of generous and luminous consciousness.

Certainly many people in our country do respect the spiritual intellect in these last decades. But in the meantime, business has effectively become the government and now rules American life on all levels, even to choosing the presidential candidates and allowing them currency. Business derives from

I

the practical intellect, works out of it, judges by it; and our government shows less evidence of generosity now than at any time in American history.

Much of the literature that the United States produces in 1995 is not generous. The culture reveals a huge anger against children. It is as if the adults envy children their closeness to the Nature we have rejected. Every year the government and private attitude toward children is meaner.

European culture in the seventeenth century dug a cellar into which the messy parts of the universe, among them pagans, Asians, Africans, and women, could be put. Now we have to say that the United States has put children in that cellar as well.

Television watchers find disintegrating human consciousness more engrossing than the intelligence of generous minds, and the ups and downs of business more engrossing than the intensities of culture. If we do love spiritual intellect and the soul of the world, we need to resist the forces that want to dishonor Nature. The consciousness of Nature now is more generous than ours.

Robert Bly
1995

An Introductory Note

W HEN SIERRA CLUB BOOKS asked me to do this anthology, I
had in mind a simple collection of poems relating to ecology.
Poets have been involved in ecology since long before the word
became current. Then, as I thought over the idea, I decided to
begin at the eighteenth century, when the poets were least inter-
ested in nature. It was the peak of human arrogance. Bushes were
clipped to resemble carriages, poets dismissed the intensity and
detail of nature and talked instead of idealizations or "goddesses,"
empires were breeding, the pride in human reason deformed all
poetry and culture. The conviction that nature is defective be-
cause it lacks reason I've called the "Old Position," and I begin
this book with seven poems of condescension, reflecting an eigh-
teenth century attitude and much in line with Descartes' state-
ment, "I think, therefore I am."

By the end of that century, an explosive reaction had taken
shape. Some German and French poets mounted an angry attack
on this pride in single consciousness, the smugness of human
reason. This storm of anger, oddly, was later called "Romanti-
cism." The German poets, chiefly Hölderlin, Novalis, and Goethe,
felt the anger most and were willing to grapple with the Old
Position ideas; the French poets, particularly Gérard de Nerval,
did well there also. Seeing Romanticism only through the poems
of the English Romantics is misleading; much of the intellectual
excitement—except in Blake—is missing. The German poets de-
veloped a sensual, elusive, augmentative, argumentative, musical,
suggestive, resonant language for their attacks. I was astonished,
translating, to realize how much of the associative point of view

3

that Freud and Jung would develop was born then. The German and French response to the Old Position, from which there are examples in Part Two, I imagine as an enormous upwelling of water, and that water is still fresh and drinkable. When one reads Novalis and Goethe, the ancient union of the day intelligence of the human being and the night intelligence of nature become audible, palpable again. It is a great advance. Of course, in other areas of European culture—pragmatic science, utilitarianism, Protestant dogmatism—the Old Position simply went on without interruption. Descartes' ideas act so as to withdraw consciousness from the non-human area, isolating the human being in his house, until, seen from the window, rocks, sky, trees, crows seem empty of energy, but especially empty of divine energy. The Novalis vision and the Descartes vision ran side by side through the nineteenth century, and Freud inherited both. He inherited respect for the integrity of nature, which sustains the Sierra Club still, and he inherited "scientific" reductionism, which longs to flood the Grand Canyon behind a concrete dam.

For the third part of this anthology I chose twenty-seven poems written roughly from 1900 to 1945, so one could see how the Novalis vision of the integrity of nature fared during those years. Some poets—Rilke is especially inventive in this area—developed a poem in which the human consciousness, though present, becomes transparent. Through it a panther appears and glows behind the words. Frost's power lies here; in poems like "The Most of It," we feel that power.

Continuing, I chose for Part Four fifty-two poems written in the last thirty years, mostly poems written in North America, but including some Russian, Greek, French, Scandinavian, and Latin American poetry also, since the struggle to open the consciousness-door that the Descartes mentality closed is taking place all over the West.

As people begin again to invest some of their trust in objects, handmade or wild, and physicists begin to suspect that objects, even down to the tiniest molecular particles, may have awareness of each other as well as "intention," *things* once more become interesting. Some marvelous object poems have been written since 1900, and in the fifth section I include a selection of those. The thing poem is a new kind of poem for the West, unseen since the old Germanic riddle poems, and the genre already includes some masterpieces.

In the last section I wanted to suggest a certain unity of consciousness that we haven't arrived at yet. All of us, since the rise of technology, have been torn into parts so often that we can hardly grasp what an interior unity could be. High school rips body and mind apart, science rips the perceiver and the thing perceived apart, the Industrial Revolution rips man and woman apart, rips father and son apart, racism rips soul and mind apart, imperialism rips the governors and the governed apart, our firm houses separate weather and person. So I've chosen a few poems from other cultures in which I sense a deeper union than the post-Industrial Revolution psyche has yet achieved. I've included Eskimo, Ojibway, Zuni poems here, early Anglo-Saxon poetry, and some medieval ballads. All of them grant nature an enormous amount of consciousness. I've also included poems by the thirteenth-century Sufi poet, Rumi, the fifteenth-century north Indian poet, Kabir, and the great woman poet of India, Mirabai. In their work we sense how many obstacles there are to unity, how many "baffles" civilization puts between human beings and nature, and yet the unity is still present. In Mirabai, at least at moments, we sense a unity inside the personality as well as a unity of the human psyche and nature.

☒   ☒   ☒

The term "version," used with four or five poems brought over from Asian languages, means that I did not translate the poem directly from the Asian language, but adapted it from several other English translations which I trust. It is not satisfactory, but the best I could do. I've also used one of Andrew Hoyem's versions of a Gérard de Nerval poem.

Part one:
The old position

The proper study of mankind is man.

Alexander Pope

WHEN DESCARTES, on November 10, 1619, developed his famous sentence, "I think, therefore I am," he intended consciously to say something liberating: I think, therefore I am not merely a solipsist. But Europe wanted to hear something else. It wanted its pride in human reason to be given philosophical underpinning. Europe had for a long time felt inferior—first to Roman culture, then to Holy culture. What I've called the Old Position puts human reason, and so human beings, in the superior position. The Old Position may be summed up, or oversimplified, this way: Consciousness is human, and involves reason. A serious gap exists between us and the rest of nature. Nature is to be watched, pitied, and taken care of if it behaves.

I don't at all mean to say that this position began with Descartes. It probably has existed since conceptualization began, perhaps even earlier. But one feels that human beings' sense that they were superior to nature was no larger than a sliver in Stone Age times. In ancient Greece, the Eleusinian Mysteries embodied resistance to human domination of nature. What took place in the Mysteries remained secret, but it is known that the experience opened the human being to other worlds. The phrase, "As above, so below" declares that the terms superior and inferior are unreal. The Mysteries evoked an awe toward matter, a sense that we shared a consciousness with plants, animals, and stones, and that all of

8

these shared a consciousness with the "soul of the world" or "soul of the globe." The longing to defeat nature no doubt grew rapidly as the city-state developed. Henry Corbin, in his books contrasting Greek and Arab thought, makes clear that Aristotle's thought presides over a reappearance of the Old Position in the ancient world, a sort of reemerging peak. Aristotle's *Analytics*, which Blake compared to a skeleton, pulls the "hard" out of nature, and isolates it.

The Church at the start of the Christian era didn't know whether to accept the ancient view that we share consciousness with nature, or to declare a new era. The Church Fathers were afraid to open the door to too many visions for fear the ancient world would simply flood the Church. As it happened, the Church rejected the Mysteries, smashed the temples, destroyed the re-lating texts and lost the doctrines. Later a few Christian geniuses and heretics fought hard, using the language of alchemy, to reassert the Mysteries vision. One, Jacob Boehme, founded his theology on the idea that there is a consciousness inside nature; he was driven out of his town by the local Protestant priest. The French priest Bossuet, writing at about the same time as Descartes, ex-pressed in this passage one of the more prevalent Christian atti-tudes toward nature:

> *May the earth be cursed, may the earth be cursed, a thousand times be cursed because from it that heavy fog and those black vapors continually rise that ascend from the dark passions and hide heaven and its light from us and draw down the lightning of God's justice against the corruption of the human race.*

This attitude was acceptable to the Church Fathers and to de-veloping capitalism. When we deny there is consciousness in nature, we also deny consciousness to the worlds we find by going *through* nature; and we end with only one world, the world of MacDonald's, and that one is exploitable. On the whole, the Church encouraged this attitude, and by 1600 the boat of the Old Position was carrying many people.

Descartes added an internal combustion engine to the movement when he declared, "I think, therefore I am." Many Europeans interpreted this to mean that since thought was confined to human beings, objects and creatures in some important way *were not*. Europe then, by whatever means, for whatever reason, over the two hundred years following Descartes' sentence, began to let the cloak of unconsciousness descend over the "inferior orders." It was lowered first over the mute areas of nature, that is, stones, vegetation. Later the mechanists and dogmatists extended it to animals, which some ancient cultures found holy. (There is a suggestion in the manger story that early Christianity also did.) By 1750 or so animals are considered to be without consciousness. The people longing to do vivisection, barred by the ancient concept that an animal had a soul, which the Catholic Church, to its credit, carried throughout the Middle Ages, sighed with relief. Now they could get on with it.

I sense during the late Middle Ages a great struggle going on in relation to women. Where did women belong? With the beings of consciousness, men and angels, or with the animals? During the period of the Grail legends, centering around *Parzival* and the year 1200, and the era of the Provençal love-song, from about 1100 to 1250, women were often experienced as carriers of consciousness, and even as creators of it. But both movements were defeated, the second destroyed by the Albigensian Crusade, when thousands of people in Provence were burned to death in their cities. Women then began the long descent. It appears that in the male psyche, women, earth and the unconscious form a sort of constellation, or triangle. Usually the attitude a man has toward one extends without his being aware of it, by secret underground channels, to the others. Thus Swift's poem, "A Gentle Echo on Women," which flatly encourages men to beat women, clearly reflects his attitude toward nature.

The eighteenth century attitude represents the culmination of a slow retreat from the open channels to nature taught by the

Mysteries and by the ancient world in general. And in the eigh-
teenth century there is a general disdaining of nature. Pope de-
clared, "The proper study of mankind is man." Johnson jokingly
asked why anyone would want to live out of London. Around
1815, Wordsworth wrote:

> Now, it is remarkable that, excepting the nocturnal Reverie of Lady
> Winchelsea, and a passage or two in the Windsor Forest of Pope, the
> poetry of the period intervening between the publication of Paradise Lost
> and the Seasons does not contain a single new image of external nature;
> and scarcely presents a familiar one from which it can be inferred that
> the eye of the Poet had been steadily fixed upon his object, much less that
> his feelings had urged him to work upon it in the spirit of genuine
> imagination. To what a low state knowledge of the most obvious and
> important phenomena had sunk, is evident from the style in which
> Dryden has executed a description of Night in one of his Tragedies, and
> Pope his translation of the celebrated moonlight scene in the Iliad.
> A blind man, in the habit of attending accurately to descriptions casu-
> ally dropped from the lips of those around him, might easily depict
> these appearances with more truth.

> CORTES alone in a night gown:
>> All things are hush'd as Nature's self lay dead;
>> The mountains seem to nod their drowsy head.
>> The little birds in dreams their songs repeat,
>> And sleeping Flowers beneath the Night-dew sweat:
>> Even lust and Envy sleep; yet love denies
>> Rest to my soul and slumber to my eyes.
>
>> Dryden's Indian Emperor

> Dryden's lines are vague, bombastic, and senseless; those of Pope,
> though he had Homer to guide him, are throughout false and contradic-
> tory. The verses of Dryden, once highly celebrated, are forgotten; those
> of Pope still retain their hold upon public estimation,—nay, there is
> not a passage of descriptive poetry, which at this day finds so many and
> such ardent admirers. Strange to think of an enthusiast, as may have
> been the case with thousands, reciting these verses under the cope of a
> moonlight sky, without having his raptures in the least disturbed by a
> suspicion of their absurdity! If these two distinguished writers could
> habitually think that the visible universe was of so little consequence

If the details of nature were not worth observing closely, we can expect that the psyche of women will not receive much attention either. The cellar of consciousness opens to receive both. Then, with the rise of imperialism, Asians and Africans are put in to keep them company. The people of Asia and Africa, who lived in a closer union with nature than the Europeans, were perceived by them as living in some state of unconsciousness, as animals are imagined to do. As soon as the cellar is full, the work of Empire can seriously begin. Holland, Spain, England, Germany compete with each other in condescension toward Asian and African religions, and compliment each other on their invasions. I'm not saying that Cartesian ideas caused invasions; there were invasions long before Descartes; but that the formulation, "I think, therefore I am," has political meaning, and made things easier for King Leopold, General Custer, and the Boston Puritans who traded in slaves.

Because I have oversimplified the Old Position so far, it may appear that only stupid people could believe it. On the contrary, many intelligent men and women have held that view for centuries, and hold it still. Distinct intellectual viewpoints are possible within this position. The viewpoints share a certain lofty attitude toward nature, often expressed by imagining hierarchies inside nature, with man at the top. A favorite device among literary people is to regard nature as a storehouse of symbols. The person who does this does not experience the tree or the pelican first as a tree or a pelican, but forces it to labor right away as a symbol. The Church Fathers were good at it. Kenneth Rexroth a few years ago wrote a sort of joke poem for his daughter on that subject:

St. Thomas Aquinas thought
That vultures were lesbians
And fertilized by the wind.
If you seek the facts of life,
Papist intellectuals
Can be very misleading.

I don't mean that the Catholic Church alone teaches this con-
descension: the Protestants teach it vigorously. Most high schools
in the United States teach it without being aware of it. The Old
Position has its own language, heavily dependent on the rational
lobe, and involves abstraction, the use of true-false questions, so-
ciological jargon, the search for symbols in poems and myths, and
learning that takes place within rigid rules. Politicians use the
language, as well as many ecologists. When an ecologist says, "The
maximum input we can have of non-organic materials before the
system reaches its saturation point is about 30%," he is using Old
Position language. In such language the body is exiled, the soul
evaporated, the mind given executive power.

I've begun this anthology with some poems from the eighteenth
century, which represents a peak of Old Position power. By 1760,
a hundred and fifty years after Descartes, the condescension has
arrived even to the poets. We can notice it in "The Three King-
doms of Nature," by Lessing, a German poet who was very pop-
ular in his day. In the poem, ego divides nature into horizontal
layers. The poem is charming and the tone optimistic.

The poetry of this time has a persistent optimism, which ex-
tends even to tragedy. A German poet, Gellert, in a poem called
"The Blind Man and the Cripple" written around 1755, discusses
the problem of a man who is blind and angry meeting another
whose legs are crippled and who also is angry. It turns out that
neither need feel grief, nor will the disaster each has experienced
bring them closer to wounded animals or to the poor. Gellert points
out that the thing is solved if the crippled man climbs on the blind
man's shoulders.

The gifts you have, the others don't;
What you don't have, some others do.
So from the world's imperfection
The social good, then, springs.

If other people didn't find missing
The gifts that Nature chose for me,
Then each person would be self-sufficient,
And what I need, no one would see.

Don't pester the gods with complaints!
The benefits which they deny to you
And grant to others, in common should be.
All we need is sociability.

There is something chilling in the last sentence. It says that if the Africans are blind, that's all right. We'll just climb on their back. As Europeans, we may be crippled, but that's all right. "All we need is sociability." If the Africans will only be sociable with the Germans, and the Dutch and the English, then we needn't worry about consciousness. Their "blindness" will be good for all of us. And the Europeans will get a good ride. Schubart's "Song of the Cape of Good Hope," written as the Germans were just beginning to invade Africa is embarrassing to read now for its optimism, and it is now left out of most German anthologies. One laughs at the wrong places.

And when the officers and men
Leap safe and sound on shore,
Then all of us will sing and shout
"At last we are in Africa!"
And we all will dance and sing.

Turning to England, we see the same mad optimism in Pope. To examine any object of nature intensely is absurd, a waste of time:

Why has not Man a microscopic eye?
For this plain reason, Man is not a Fly.

He is perfectly satisfied with the way seeing and blindness are distributed in the universe.

Without this just gradation, could they be
Subjected, these to those, or all to thee?

One notices that the word "they" in the first line could apply to natives or women, as well as to still lower links in the chain of being. His lines of disdain for the American Indian ("Lo, the poor Indian") is interesting in that the main evidence of inferiority that Pope mentions in the Indian is that he sees the divine in clouds and wind. To Pope that is intolerable. Swift expresses a similar disdain for the consciousness of women.

What most moves women when we them address?
A dress.

Some women have revealed that it is a man's psyche that moves them; Swift says no, consciousness is not involved. To move a woman, buy her a dress. Woman can be bought; when bought she will be "a dear."

But deer have horns: how must I keep her under?
Keep her under.

He complains that women, no doubt from lack of consciousness, are inconstant.

If she be wind, what stills her when she blows?
Blows.

Milton's style, twisting English syntax until it resembles Latin, expresses a curiously arrogant attitude toward the English language, and toward the unconscious, which is never allowed to speak simply. Sandra Gilbert, in *The Madwoman in the Attic: The Woman Writer and the Nineteenth-Century Literary Imagination*, has written brilliantly on Milton's half-conscious Satanizing of women; again we see the triangle concept working. In Book X of *Paradise Lost*, Milton adds something pathetic to Pope and Swift. Milton asks why women were created at all. We were doing so well with only men, he mumbles, and "this fair defect of Nature" has brought "innumerable disturbances on Earth." This is a standard complaint. Suddenly in the next few lines, all sorts of repressed material starts boiling out. It turns out that he knew a woman who refused to marry him "through her perverseness." Even worse, he found to his horror that a woman he met and liked late in life was married already to one of his enemies. These accidents of life on earth he blames all on women. Or is nature to be blamed? Or the unconscious?

As a final poem for this group, I've chosen "Dover Beach," which many readers already know and admire. I should say why I put it here. It was written a hundred years after Lessing, and to me it illustrates how long and firmly the Old Position hung on in Europe, especially in England. "Dover Beach" is marvelous in places, and its subject is precisely what we have been describing, the mental poverty and isolated sadness that comes when human beings deny consciousness to the ocean. (Once, consciousness, as Arnold sees, lay gleaming about the hills and shores precisely as the ocean now lies gleaming.) This is the poverty that comes when human beings claim all consciousness for themselves. And though Arnold has seen this state of poverty, isolation, retreat, and melancholic diminishing so clearly, the only solution he can see to it is more human contact. In Gellert's phrase, it is more "sociability" he wants.

> Ah, love, let us be true
> To one another!

And he gives as the reason why two people should be true to each other:

> for the world, which seems
> To lie before us like a land of dreams,
> So various, so beautiful, so new,
> Hath really neither joy, nor love, nor light,
> Nor certitude, nor peace, nor help for pain;

There is a lot of slander of the world here, and much self-pity of the sort we have become used to in recent American poetry.

And we are here as on a darkling plain
Swept with confused alarms of struggle and fight,
Where ignorant armies clash by night.

We say to ourselves that this *is* true of the human world; yet once more by omission the entire non-human world has been denied consciousness, or given the muddled consciousness through which armies operate at night. Arnold means human armies, not insects or nature, and yet he implies that the human being lives surrounded by chaos. Lewis Thomas would say that this view of the world is not true. Protozoa don't clash by night. They have intricate harmonies worked out, which have already lasted for millions of years. The Old Position does not see that.

While drinking, all at once I saw
Why nature's made of three realms.
Animals and people both drink and love,
Each according to its urges.
The dolphin and eagle, the flea and the dog,
Experience affection, and use their mouths.
So whatever can drink and love both,
Those in the first kingdom have their place.

Vegetation, then, makes up the second realm.
That falls far short of the higher one.
Leaves have no love, but they can drink,
When the dripping clouds sink low.
The cedar drinks, the clover drinks,
the grapevine and the aloe tree.
So whatever drinks, but cannot love,
Those in the second kingdom all belong.

The kingdom of stones makes up the third.
Diamonds we have, and also gravel.
Stones feel no thirst, no tender urges;
a stone grows without rain or love.
Well then whatever can neither drink nor love
those in the third kingdom have their place.
And, human, tell me, if you have neither
love nor wine—what are you? A stone.

GOTTHOLD LESSING / 1753
adapted by Robert Bly from the
translation of Alfred Baskerville

Up! Up! You brothers, now be strong,
The parting day is here!
It lies so heavy on the soul.
But over land and ocean we'll go
To the sands of Africa.

The ones we love stand crowded near,
Dear brothers, as we go.
So many strong ties bind us now
To our German Fatherland,
To part is heavy on the soul . . .

Farewell, my friends! Perhaps we see you
For the last time as we look.
So think that not for short time
Only does friendship last, but forever,
And God is everywhere . . .

When, at last, oh friends, the Table Mountain
Looms from the bluish mist,
Then we'll all lift up our hands
And cry with joy: Land! Brothers! Land!
And then the deck will tremble.

And when the officers and men
Leap safe and sound on shore,
Then all of us will sing and shout:
"At last we are in Africa!"
And we all will dance and sing.

We'll live from then in a distant land
As Germans brave and good,
And people far and wide will say,

What honest folk the Germans are,
They are both lively and brave.

On the Cape of Good Hope at last
We'll drink its heavenly wine.
We'll think with love and yearning,
Oh distant friends, of you,
And tears will mingle with the wine.

SCHUBART / 1850
adapted by Robert Bly from the
translation of Alfred Baskerville

20

The bliss of man (could pride that blessing find)
Is not to act or think beyond mankind;
No pow'rs of body or of soul to share,
But what his nature and his state can bear.
Why has not man a microscopic eye?
For this plain reason, man is not a fly.
Say what the use, were finer optics giv'n,
T' inspect a mite, or comprehend the heav'n' . . .

Far as creations ample range extends,
The scale of sensual, mental pow'rs ascends:
Mark how it mounts, to man's imperial race,
From the green myriads in the peopled grass. . . .

How instinct varies in the grov'ling swine,
Compar'd, half-reas'ning elephant, with thine!
'Twixt that, and reason, what a nice barrier;
Forever sep'rate, yet forever near!
Remembrance and reflection how allied;
What thin partitions sense from thought divide:
And middle natures, how they long to join,
Yet never pass th' insuperable line!
Without this just gradation, could they be
Subjected, these to those, or all to thee?
The pow'rs of all subdu'd by thee alone,
Is not thy reason all these pow'rs in one?

ALEXANDER POPE / 1733
from *An Essay on Man*

Lo, the poor Indian! whose untutor'd mind
Sees God in clouds, or hears him in the wind;
His soul, proud Science never taught to stray
Far as the solar walk, or milky way;
Yet simple Nature to his hope has giv'n,
Behind the cloud-topp'd hill, an humbler heav'n;
Some safer world in depth of woods embrac'd,
Some happier island in the wat'ry waste,
Where slaves once more their native land behold,
No fiends torment, no Christians thirst for gold.
To be, contents his natural desire,
He asks no angel's wing, no seraph's fire;
But thinks, admitted to that equal sky,
His faithful dog shall bear him company.

ALEXANDER POPE / 1733
from *An Essay on Man*

In the Doric Manner

Shepherd: Echo, I ween, will in the wood reply,
And quaintly answer questions: shall I try?
                    Echo: Try.
What must we do our passion to express?
                    Press.
How shall I please her, who ne'er loved before?
                    Be Fore.
What most moves women when we them address?
                    A dress.
Say, what can keep her chaste whom I adore?
                    A door.
If music softens rocks, love tunes my lyre.
                    Liar.
Then teach me, Echo, how shall I come by her?
                    Buy her.
When bought, no question I shall be her dear?
                    Her deer.
But deer have horns: how must I keep her under?
                    Keep her under.
But what can glad me when she's laid on bier?
                    Beer.
What must I do when women will be kind?
                    Be kind.
What must I do when women will be cross?
                    Be cross.
Lord, what is she that can so turn and wind?
                    Wind.
If she be wind, what stills her when she blows?
                    Blows.
But if she bang again, still should I bang her?
                    Bang her.

Is there no way to moderate her anger?
                    Hang her.
Thanks, gentle Echo! right thy answers tell
What woman is and how to guard her well.
                    Guard her well.

JONATHAN SWIFT / C.1700

24

"Oh, why did God,
Creator wise, that peopled highest Heaven
With Spirits masculine, create at last
This novelty on Earth, this fair defect
Of Nature, and not fill the World at once
With men as Angels, without feminine;
Or find some other way to generate
Mankind? This mischief had not then befall'n,
And more that shall befall—innumerable
Disturbances on Earth through female snares,
And strait conjunction with this sex: for either
He never shall find out fit mate, but such
As some misfortune brings him, or mistake;
Or whom he wishes most shall seldom gain,
Through her perverseness, but shall see her gained
By a far worse, or, if she love, withheld
By parents; or his happiest choice too late
Shall meet, already linked and wedlock-bound
To a fell adversary, his hate or shame:
Which infinite calamity shall cause
To human life, and household peace confound."

JOHN MILTON / 1667
from *Paradise Lost*

The sea is calm to-night.
The tide is full, the moon lies fair
Upon the straits;—on the French coast the light
Gleams and is gone; the cliffs of England stand,
Glimmering and vast, out in the tranquil bay.
Come to the window, sweet is the night-air!
Only, from the long line of spray
Where the sea meets the moon-blanch'd land,
Listen! you hear the grating roar
Of pebbles which the waves draw back, and fling,
At their return, up the high strand,
Begin, and cease, and then again begin,
With tremulous cadence slow, and bring
The eternal note of sadness in.

Sophocles long ago
Heard it on the Ægæan, and it brought
Into his mind the turbid ebb and flow
Of human misery; we
Find also in the sound a thought,
Hearing it by this distant northern sea.

The Sea of Faith
Was once, too, at the full, and round earth's shore
Lay like the folds of a bright girdle furl'd.
But now I only hear
Its melancholy, long, withdrawing roar,
Retreating, to the breath
Of the night-wind, down the vast edges drear
And naked shingles of the world.

Ah, love, let us be true
To one another! for the world, which seems

To lie before us like a land of dreams,
So various, so beautiful, so new,
Hath really neither joy, nor love, nor light,
Nor certitude, nor peace, nor help for pain;
And we are here as on a darkling plain
Swept with confused alarms of struggle and flight,
Where ignorant armies clash by night.

MATTHEW ARNOLD / 1867

Part two:
The attack on
the old position

Now I a fourfold vision see,
And a fourfold vision is given to me;
'Tis fourfold in my supreme delight
And threefold in soft Beulah's night
And twofold always. May God us keep
From Single vision & Newton's sleep!

William Blake
November 22, 1802

Around 1800 an explosive attack on the Old Position began. This outburst is usually called Romanticism, but that word implies too much gentleness. When one reads the major texts, especially in German and French, one sees that the ground tone is anger. Gérard de Nerval and Hölderlin were angry at the betrayal of ordinary life involved in the eighteenth-century condescension toward nature. Gérard de Nerval said:

> Free thinker, do you think you are the only thinker
> on this earth in which life blazes inside all things?
> Your liberty does what it wishes with the powers it controls,
> but when you gather to plan, the universe is not there.

Hölderlin, referring to the sort of poems Pope wrote in his visits to the country, where the Roman gods stood about in formal gardens, said:

> I'm sick of you hypocrites, babbling about gods!
> Rationality is what you have, you don't believe
> In Helios, nor the sea being, nor the thunder being;
> And the earth is a corpse, so why thank her?

Gérard de Nerval sensed that a genuine channel was about to open up between the European and the ancient Greek gods, and he wanted to be not sanctimonious or hypocritical, but religious.

He understood that if the channel opened again, a lot of things would collapse:

Underneath the Arch of Constantine a swarthy sybil slumbers.
When she awakes the gate will crumble.

In Germany, Goethe, Hölderlin and Novalis led the attack, and we get quite a different sense of the whole thing from them than we get from the English Romantics. All three handle ideas. Each puts up ideas that meet, even angrily confront, the Descartian system. In *Dichtung und Wahrheit*, Goethe described his reaction, and his university friends', when they first saw the Cartesian system in print: "It seemed to us so gray, monstrous and death-like that we could hardly stand it; we shuddered as if facing a ghost." The Germans then allowed their anger to flow into concepts, and took part in the battle of ideas. The English Romantics, with the exception of Blake, remained primarily in the realm of feeling. They feel the ideas but they don't think them.

Novalis was the name taken by a young German named Friedrich von Hardenberg. He was born in 1772. When he was twenty-three or so he fell in love deeply with a young woman, Sophie, and had what Jung would call an *anima* experience; through that his whole feminine side opened up to him, as well as the richness of dreams, the mystery of transformation, the power of night. The young woman died two years later, and he wrote his *Hymns to the Night*, an amazing book in which all that has been ignored in Europe for centuries is praised: the unconscious is praised, night, sleep, sexuality, and woman. I've translated here the prose poem version of the Second Hymn (he wrote each poem as a prose poem and also as a lined poem). Novalis himself did not live long, but before he died he set down a number of aphorisms opposing Descartes' ideas, some of which I've included here (the lines from *Pollen* and *Fragments*). Though there is no link between Novalis and Blake, it is surprising how closely Novalis' aphorisms, written exactly in 1800, resemble Blake's, especially in his insistence that the human body is a temple. It is not the mind that is the temple; the temple is what we share with the animals. "Man is a sun and his senses are the planets." Novalis says in effect that to break the Old Position we will have to study the outer world, study plants and animals and insects. The human soul he implies is not "inside" the human being; it is not an immortal part given by God at birth, far inside; rather the seat of the soul is where the inner world and the outer world meet. "Where they overlap, it is in every point of the overlap."

Goethe, as we know, spent hours and years in precise observation of plants, and became one of the most gifted naturalists in Europe. All during this time, wild material flowed into his poems as if from the Mysteries. So "the sober" and "the spontaneous" do not cancel each other out. These stanzas are from "The Holy Longing":

> Distance does not make you falter,
> now, arriving in magic, flying,
> and, finally, insane for the light,
> you are the butterfly and you are gone.
>
> And so long as you haven't experienced
> this: to die and so to grow,
> you are only a troubled guest
> on the dark earth.

Blake is the strongest of the English Romantics in confronting the Old Position ideas. He begins his attack by suggesting that angels have to be looked at over again. Angels believe in the Old Position, perhaps because they have no body. In the long prose poem of Blake's I've included here, called "A Memorable Fancy," the angel Blake talks with is linked to Aristotle. Blake does not forgive Christianity for making an alliance with Aristotle's metaphysics. The Angel typically threatens Blake with hell if he thinks any new thoughts. Blake however challenges the Aristotelian angel to show him the place Blake will occupy in eternity if it is so bad. An interesting narrative follows. The Aristotelian angel leads Blake through a stable to a church vault to a mill to a cave to a point overlooking the nothingness of a parking lot or a condominium in Colorado. The void is full of hostile energies, spiders, serpents and tigers, and fearful unconscious material. But when Blake stops reading Aristotle and the Church Fathers, he finds himself on a pleasant bank, hearing harp music.

Blake then goes back to the mill, finds an Angel, and tells him what *his* lot in eternity will be. He takes the angel, flies through the stars, enters the stable and the church, passes through the Bible and ends at brick buildings, where they see monkeys in chains. The primitive part of each human being is being ripped off and eaten, by others and by himself. When the meat is all gone and the skeleton left, the skeleton turns out to be Aristotle's *Analytics*. Blake's book *The Marriage of Heaven and Hell*, to which this prose poem belongs, is surely one of the greatest works of English literature, and it is organized brilliantly as an attack on Aquinas, Pope, Reynolds, Aristotle and the makers of Empire.

Keats' tone is more like Goethe's, though the issue of the consciousness we share with nature is not really discussed. In "Ode to the Nightingale" he does not hear much melancholy or awareness of death in the nightingale's song. It seems to Keats, having just come from his brother's deathbed, that only human beings have that consciousness. At the last minute Keats turns back to the human world, somewhat as Matthew Arnold later did. One can't say either man was wrong, but Goethe somehow remains true to shared consciousness; one feels that Goethe would have jumped into the forest, confident he could find his way back later.

In his bravery, Goethe goes about three steps beyond Pope. Goethe sees a consciousness in nature, and he doesn't dismiss it as the intuition of an untutored mind. He goes toward it. Then he takes the next step, which is understanding that all consciousness has a dangerous side, and that if there is a consciousness in nature, it too has a dangerous side. His poem "The Invisible King" is frightening. The boy and his father—the love-unit I think has been most damaged by the Industrial Revolution—are traveling together. The boy sees in the groves "the invisible king" and then

33

his daughters, but the adult father does not. The father in a rationalist's way dismisses the boy's questions.

"Calm down, my boy, no need for all this—
It's dry oak leaves making noise in the wind."

. . . . .

"I see the spot very clearly, my boy—
an old gray willow, that's all there is."

We sense how many European and American fathers have done that to their sons; the poem says that the rationalist viewpoint simply opens the boy further to the dark side of consciousness, and the poem ends with the boy dead in the father's arms.

As I struggled with the poem, trying to translate it, I realized that many writers of medieval ballads, with their motif of the woman or child stolen by the "other people" were granting consciousness to trees and land. It was their way of saying it. A poet can say it directly, as Pythagoras did, "Everything is intelligent!" or say it by a narrative. I'll return to this idea in the last section of this book.

The whole question of whether the consciousness of nature, as well as human beings, has a dark side, becomes a crucial issue. We notice that Keats, though he was so acute about human misery, in general, like Wordsworth, idealized nature. If the triangle concept I spoke of in the preceding essay is correct, that would mean Keats also idealized women and the unconscious. We notice that in the second stanza of "To Autumn," autumn becomes a woman, and that woman is sweet, lackadaisical, gentle, patient, apparently without anger. The English Romantics—Blake again is an exception—seem to have had no way of visualizing the possibility that the consciousness of nature has a dark side. Wordsworth in the rowing passage of the *Prelude* senses it, but doesn't bring it into concept. He feels it, but doesn't think it. The Hindu civilization conceptualized the dark side of the consciousness "out there" as Kali, the "death-goddess," whom they visualized as a vigorous female, wearing a necklace of skulls, dancing on the body of a sort of world-man. Goethe's "The Invisible King" suggests that if a culture refuses to see the Kali energy, it then leaves an open invasion route. Keats at the end of his life saw the Kali energy approaching in "La Belle Dame Sans Merci," but for him it was too late.

I would say the American Romantic poets, Whitman, Dickinson, Thoreau, follow the Keats path more than the Goethe path. It is difficult for them to imagine a dark side of the shared consciousness, or difficult to imagine it vividly.

As for the French poets, most did not follow Gérard de Nerval's lead as he brooded on the terrific hostile power of the Greek gods and goddesses. I've translated a few lines from Alfred de Vigny, who does. De Vigny goes so far as to try to protect human beings from nature. He grants nature enormous power, and he sees that her power is connected somehow with the power of one's own personal mother. De Vigny does not love nature. He is afraid of nature. He understands that in order to love nature, a man has to have overcome the fear of his own mother. He has to have faced the incest complex that Sophocles talks of, dealt with it somehow. The dark side of nature will invade the man who has an unconscious union with his mother. Such a man will lose his "eyes," the light of consciousness, as Oedipus did.

The poetry of the so-called Romantics contains many references to the call one form of consciousness makes to another, a call either answered or not. Goethe's "Mignon" is one of the most mysterious of these "call" poems. The poem says that we have to take a journey out somewhere, away from ourselves, but in the three stanzas the person spoken to changes from a "beloved" or "darling" to a loving protector to a "father." That is an odd sequence. Moreover, the place he imagines changes—in the first stanza it is a sort of celestial place suggesting the ancient civilization of the Mediterranean, with Apollo, yet it takes on some aspect of a Christian heaven—archetypal, as Jung would say. In the second stanza, the place has become a house or mansion built by human

35

beings, though still built in a Mediterranean style, with pillars and statues. Some fear begins to enter, I don't know why.

By the third stanza the place has moved north, perhaps to the Alps; there are mountains, mules, a lot of fog, danger, and dragons. Dragons usually suggest unconscious energies. Dragons are dangerous enough, but, even worse, these are asleep. However, Goethe says that this last place is where we have to go, the road we are on leads there whether we want to go there or not, and he says that our companion will apparently be our own father.

This "father" could be the wise old man of fairy tales. It seems encouraging for Europe that the masculine psyche is now considered to be a possible guide to the dark world. The male guide is not replacing the feminine psyche, which has for centuries been such a guide, but the poem seems to suggest that it is being added to the feminine psyche. It's possible the poem also moves historically from the Greek world to French spirituality to Germanic alchemy. I feel however that the whole thing is more unconscious than that, and that Goethe himself is not sure why one image follows another.

I hope that readers of the German and French translations will look up the poems in the original languages. The German poems especially repay study. Translating Novalis' "Second Hymn to the Night" and Hölderlin's "Bread and Wine, Part 7," I was continually amazed at the ability of the German, written down by these two men in 1798 and 1800, to suggest, using ambiguities, prefixes and resonances, the same associations around sleep, sexuality, night-consciousness, and dream that Freud later pointed out in elegant but knotted prose. No poet in English could do that in 1800. The *Songs of Innocence and Experience* approach it. But Novalis and Hölderlin have some huge sweetness; they don't point fingers like Blake; they write some immense music instead, listening we want to weep. Listening to this music we understand that our sexual nature has been seen, our contemporary aliveness has been seen, our weakness in imagination has been seen, our spiritual thirst—so intense—has been seen. Postindustrial psychology began with Freud and Jung and their friends, all of whom wrote in German, not English. I understood as I translated Novalis that the reason for that was because they read in German, that is, at eighteen their brains were stirred and fertilized by the reso- nances present in the poems written a hundred years earlier by Novalis, Hölderlin and Goethe.

GOLDEN LINES

"Astonishing! Everything is intelligent!"
    Pythagoras

Free thinker! Do you think you are the only thinker
on this earth in which life blazes inside all things?
Your liberty does what it wishes with the powers it controls,
but when you gather to plan, the universe is not there.

Look carefully in an animal at a spirit alive;
every flower is a soul opening out into nature;
a mystery touching love is asleep inside metal.
"Everything is intelligent!" And everything moves you.

In that blind wall, look out for the eyes that pierce you:
the substance of creation cannot be separated from a word . . .
Do not force it to labor in some low phrase!

Often a Holy Thing is living hidden in a dark creature;
and like an eye which is born covered by its lids,
a pure spirit is growing strong under the bark of stones!

GÉRARD DE NERVAL / 1854
translated by Robert Bly

I'm sick of you hypocrites babbling about gods!
   Rationality is what you have, you don't believe
      In Helios, nor the sea being, nor the thunder being;
         And the earth is a corpse, so why thank her?

As for you gods, be calm! You are decorations in their poems,
   Even though the energy has drained out of your names.
      And, Mother of Nature, if a word with immense
         energy is needed, people remember yours.

FRIEDRICH HÖLDERLIN / 1798
translated by Robert Bly

All Bibles or sacred codes have been the causes of the following Errors:

  1. That Man has two real existing principles Viz: a Body & a Soul.

  2. That Energy, call'd Evil, is alone from the Body, & that Reason, call'd Good, is alone from the Soul.

  3. That God will torment Man in Eternity for following his Energies.

But the following Contraries to these are True:

  1. Man has no Body distinct from his Soul for that call'd Body is a portion of Soul discern'd by the five Senses, the chief inlets of Soul in this age.

  2. Energy is the only life and is from the Body and Reason is the bound or outward circumference of Energy.

  3. Energy is Eternal Delight.

WILLIAM BLAKE / 1793
from *The Marriage of Heaven and Hell*

As I was walking among the fires of hell, delighted with the enjoyments of Genius, which to Angels look like torment and insanity, I collected some of their Proverbs; thinking that as the sayings used in a nation mark its character, so the Proverbs of Hell shew the nature of Infernal Wisdom better than any description of buildings or garments.

When I came home: on the abyss of the five senses, where a flat sided steep frowns over the present world, I saw a mighty Devil folded in black clouds, hovering on the sides of the rock, with corroding fires he wrote the following sentence now perceived by the minds of men, & read by them on earth:

> How do you know but ev'ry Bird that cuts the airy way,
> Is an immense world of delight, clos'd by your senses five?

WILLIAM BLAKE / 1793
from *The Marriage of Heaven and Hell*

When geometric diagrams and digits
Are no longer the keys to living things,
When people who go about singing or kissing
Know deeper things than the great scholars,
When society is returned once more
To unimprisoned life, and to the universe,
And when light and darkness mate
Once more and make something entirely transparent,
And people see in poems and fairy tales
The true history of the world,
Then our entire twisted nature will turn
And run when a single secret word is spoken.

NOVALIS / 1800
translated by Robert Bly

DELFICA

Remember that old love song, Daphne? the one that
    always began again where we left off:
"At the foot of a sycamore, or under white laurels, or
    below the olive, or beneath myrtles, or covered over
    by a weeping willow tree . . ."

Remember the temple with huge columns?
Can you still taste those sour lemons?
You were so blond you cut your teeth on those
    yellow skins.
Could you recognize that dangerous grotto wherein
    sleep the dragon's seeds?

The gods you weep for will return as ghosts.
The old order of ancient days shall reestablish itself.
Earthquakes prophesy the revolution.

Underneath the Arch of Constantine a swarthy sybil
    slumbers.
When she awakes the gate will crumble.

GÉRARD DE NERVAL / 1845
version by Andrew Hoyem

The natural world is a spiritual house, where the pillars, that
   are alive,
let slip at times some strangely garbled words;
Man walks there through forests of physical things that are
   also spiritual things,
that watch him with affectionate looks.

As the echoes of great bells coming from a long way off
become entangled in a deep and profound association,
a merging as huge as night, or as huge as clear light,
odors and colors and sounds all mean—each other.

Perfumes exist that are cool as the flesh of infants,
fragile as oboes, green as open fields,
and others exist also, corrupt, dense, and triumphant,

having the suggestions of infinite things,
such as musk and amber, myrrh and incense,
that describe the voyages of the body and soul.

CHARLES BAUDELAIRE / 1856?
translated by Robert Bly

THE SECOND POEM THE NIGHT-WALKER WROTE

Over all the hilltops
Silence,
Among all the treetops
You feel hardly
A breath moving.
The birds fall silent in the woods.
Simply wait! Soon
You too will be silent.

GOETHE / 1780
translated by Robert Bly

"ALL THE FRUIT . . ."

All the fruit is ripe, plunged in fire, cooked,
And they have passed their test on earth, and one law is this:
That everything curls inward, like snakes,
Prophetic, dreaming on
The hills of heaven. And many things
Have to stay on the shoulders like a load
of failure. However the roads
Are bad. For the chained elements,
Like horses, are going off to the side,
And the old
Laws of the earth. And a longing
For disintegration constantly comes. Many things however
Have to stay on the shoulders. Steadiness is essential.
Forwards, however, or backwards we will
Not look. Let us learn to live swaying
As in a rocking boat on the sea.

FRIEDRICH HÖLDERLIN / 1803
translated by Robert Bly

Oh friend, we arrived too late. The divine energies
    Are still alive, but isolated above us, in the archetypal world.
They keep on going there, and, apparently, don't bother if
    Humans live or not . . . that is a heavenly mercy.
Sometimes a human's clay is not strong enough to take the water;
    Human beings can carry the divine only sometimes.
What is living now? Night dreams of them. But craziness
    Helps, so does sleep. Grief and Night toughen us,
Until people capable of sacrifice once more rock
    In the iron cradle, desire people, as the ancients, strong enough
      for water.
In thunderstorms it will arrive. I have the feeling often, meanwhile,
    It is better to sleep, since the Guest comes so seldom;
We waste our life waiting, and I haven't the faintest idea
    How to act or talk . . . in the lean years who needs poets?
But poets as you say are like the holy disciple of the Wild One
    Who used to stroll over the fields through the whole divine
      night.

FRIEDRICH HÖLDERLIN / 1800
translated by Robert Bly

1. The seat of the soul is where the inner world and the outer world meet. Where they overlap, it is in every point of the overlap.

2. Self-expression is the source of all abasement, just as, contrariwise, it is the basis for all true elevation. The first step is introspection—exclusive contemplation of the self. But whoever stops there goes only half way. The second step must be genuine observation outward—spontaneous, sober observation of the external world.

3. The more personal, local, temporal, particularized a poem is, the nearer it stands to the *centrum* of poetry. A poem must be completely inexhaustible, like a human being or a good proverb.

4. There is only one temple in the world and that is the human body. Nothing is more sacred than that noble form.

5. A man will never achieve anything excellent in the way of representation so long as he wishes to represent nothing more than his own experiences, his own favorite objects, so long as he cannot bring himself to study with diligence and to represent at his leisure an object wholly foreign and wholly uninteresting to him.

6. Man is a sun and his senses are the planets.

NOVALIS / 1798
from *Pollen* and *Fragments*
translated by Charles E. Passage

Does morning always *have* to come? Will earthly influence *always* go on? Doing this and that is secular and smashes the holy approach of Night. And the substance Love burns on the altar, secretly, does it have to go out? Daylight has got limits and hours, but the hegemony of Night penetrates through space and through time. Sleep does not end, sleep lasts. God-like sleep: often give those obsessed with daily tasks, but inwardly mistresses of night, your joy. Only the shallow man sees nothing in your face, he knows only of the shadow-sleep, that you in human mercy throw over us in the anteroom of true night. Divine sleep, they do not know that you live in the golden ocean of the grapes, in the almond with its other-worldly oil, and in the poppy's brown substances. They have no idea that it is you who subtly embrace the breasts of the young girl, and turn her darkened cave into the Garden of Delight, and have no clue that you are the one who opening the world of delight meets us at the edge of old stories and carries in your hand the key to the mansions where the completed ones live, you are the messenger who opens mysteries that unfold forever, but avoids words.

NOVALIS / 1800
translated by Robert Bly

Hear the voice of the Bard!
Who Present, Past, & Future, sees;
Whose ears have heard
The Holy Word
That walk'd among the ancient trees,

Calling the lapsed Soul,
And weeping in the evening dew;
That might control
The starry pole,
And fallen, fallen light renew!

"O Earth, O Earth, return!
Arise from out the dewy grass;
Night is worn,
And the morn
Rises from the slumberous mass.

"Turn away no more;
Why wilt thou turn away?
The starry floor,
The wat'ry shore,
Is giv'n thee till the break of day."

WILLIAM BLAKE / 1794
from *Songs of Experience*

The roaring of the wind is my wife and the Stars through the window pane are my Children. The mighty abstract Idea I have of Beauty in all things stifles the more divided and minute domestic happiness—an amiable wife and sweet Children I contemplate as part of that Beauty, but I must have a thousand of those beautiful particles to fill up my heart. I feel more and more every day, as my imagination strengthens, that I do not live in this world alone but in a thousand worlds. No sooner am I alone than shapes of epic greatness are stationed around me, and serve my Spirit the office which is equivalent to a King's body guard—then "Tragedy with scepter'd pall, comes sweeping by." According to my state of mind I am with Achilles shouting in the Trenches, or with Theocritus in the Vales of Sicily. Or I throw my whole being into Troilus, and repeating those lines, "I wander, like a lost Soul upon the Stygian banks staying for waftage," I melt into the air with a voluptuousness so delicate that I am content to be alone.

JOHN KEATS / 1819

An Angel came to me and said: "O pitiable foolish young man! O horrible! O dreadful state! consider the hot burning dungeon thou art preparing for thyself to all eternity, to which thou art going to such career."

I said: "perhaps you will be willing to shew me my eternal lot & we will contemplate together upon it and see whether your lot or mine is most desirable."

So he took me thro' a stable thro' a church & down into the church vault, at the end of which was a mill: thro' the mill we went, and came to a cave: down the winding cavern we groped our tedious way, till a void boundless as a nether sky appear'd beneath us, & we held by the roots of trees and hung over this immensity; but I said: "if you please, we will commit ourselves to this void, and see whether providence is here also: if you will not, I will?" but he answer'd: "do not presume, O young man, but as we here remain, behold thy lot which will soon appear when the darkness passes away."

So I remain'd with him, sitting in the twisted root of an oak; he was suspended in a fungus, which hung with the head downward into the deep.

By degrees we beheld the infinite Abyss, fiery as the smoke of a burning city; beneath us, at an immense distance, was the sun, black but shining; round it were fiery tracks on which revolv'd vast spiders, crawling after their prey, which flew, or rather swum, in the infinite deep, in the most terrific shapes of animals sprung from corruption; & the air was full of them, & seem'd composed of them: these are Devils, and are called Powers of the air. I now asked my companion which was my eternal lot? he said: "between the black & white spiders."

But now, from between the black & white spiders, a cloud and fire burst and rolled thro' the deep, black'ning all beneath, so that the nether deep grew black as a sea, & rolled with a terrible noise; beneath us was nothing now to be seen but a black tempest, till looking east between the clouds & the waves, we saw a cataract of blood mixed with fire, and not many stones' throw from us appear'd and sunk again the scaly fold of a monstrous serpent; at last, to the east, distant about three degrees, appear'd a fiery crest above the waves; slowly it reared like a ridge of golden rocks, till we discover'd two globes of crimson fire, from which the sea fled away in clouds of smoke; and now we saw it was the head of Leviathan; his forehead was divided into streaks of green & purple like those on a tyger's forehead: soon we saw his mouth & red gills hang just above the raging foam, tinging the black deep with beams of blood, advancing toward us with all the fury of a spiritual existence.

My friend the Angel climb'd up from his station into the mill; I remain'd alone; & then this appearance was no more, but I found myself sitting on a pleasant bank beside a river by moonlight, hearing a harper, who sung to the harp; & his theme was: "The man who never alters his opinion is like standing water, & breeds reptiles of the mind."

But I arose and sought for the mill, & there I found my Angel, who, surprised, asked me how I escaped?

I answer'd: "All that we saw was owing to your metaphysics; for when you ran away, I found myself on a bank by moonlight hearing a harper. But now we have seen my eternal lot, shall I shew you yours? he laugh'd at my proposal; but I by force suddenly caught him in my arms; & flew westerly thro' the night, till we were elevated above the earth's shadow; then I flung myself with him directly into the body of the sun; here I clothed myself in white, & taking in my hand Swedenborg's volumes, sunk from the glorious clime, and passed all the planets till we came to saturn: here I staid to rest, & then leap'd into the void between saturn & the fixed stars.

"Here," said I, "is your lot, in this space, if space it may be call'd." Soon we saw the stable and the church, & I took him to the altar and open'd the Bible, and lo! it was a deep pit, into which I descended, driving the Angel before me; soon we saw

seven houses of brick; one we enter'd; in it were a number of
monkeys, baboons, & all of that species, chain'd by the middle,
grinning and snatching at one another, but withheld by the
shortness of their chains: however, I saw that they sometimes
grew numerous, and then the weak were caught by the strong,
and with a grinning aspect, first coupled with, & then devour'd,
by plucking off first one limb and then another, till the body
was left a helpless trunk; this, after grinning & kissing it with
seeming fondness, they devour'd too; and here & there I saw
one savourily picking the flesh off of his own tail; as the stench
terribly annoy'd us both, we went into the mill, & I in my
hand brought the skeleton of a body, which in the mill was
Aristotle's Analytics.

So the Angel said: "thy phantasy has imposed upon me, &
thou oughtest to be ashamed."

I answer'd: "we impose on one another, & it is but lost time to
converse with you whose works are only Analytics."

WILLIAM BLAKE / 1793
from *The Marriage of Heaven and Hell*

When midnight comes a host of dogs and men
Go out and track the badger to his den,
And put a sack within the hole, and lie
Till the old grunting badger passes bye.
He comes and hears—they let the strongest loose.
The old fox hears the noise and drops the goose.
The poacher shoots and hurries from the cry,
And the old hare half wounded buzzes bye.
They get a forked stick to bear him down
And clap the dogs and take him to the town,
And bait him all the day with many dogs,
And laugh and shout and fright the scampering hogs.
He runs along and bites at all he meets:
They shout and hollo down the noisy streets.
He turns about to face the loud uproar
And drives the rebels to their very door.
The frequent stone is hurled where eer they go;
When badgers fight, then every one's a foe.
The dogs are clapt and urged to join the fray;
The badger turns and drives them all away.
Though scarcely half as big, demure and small
He fights with dogs for hours and beats them all.
The heavy mastiff, savage in the fray,
Lies down and licks his feet and turns away.
The bulldog knows his match and waxes cold,
The badger grins and never leaves his hold.
He drives the crowd and follows at their heels
And bites them through—the drunkard swears and reels.

The frightened women take the boys away,
The blackguard laughs and hurries on the fray.
He tries to reach the woods, an awkward race,
But sticks and cudgels quickly stop the chase.

He turns agen and drives the noisy crowd
And beats the many dogs in noises loud.
He drives away and beats them every one,
And then they loose them all and set them on.
He falls as dead and kicked by boys and men,
Then starts and grins and drives the crowd agen;
Till kicked and torn and beaten out he lies
And leaves his hold and cackles, groans, and dies.

JOHN CLARE / 1836?

The thistledown's flying
Though the winds are all still,
On the green grass now lying,
Now mounting the hill,
The spring from the fountain
Now boils like a pot,
Through stones past the counting,
It bubbles red hot.

The ground parched and cracked is
Like overbaked bread,
The greensward all wracked is,
Bents dried up and dead.
The fallow fields glitter
Like water indeed,
And gossamers twitter,
Flung from weed unto weed.

Hill-tops like hot iron
Glitter hot i' the sun.
And the rivers we're eyeing
Burn to gold as they run.
Burning hot is the ground,
Liquid gold is the air;
Whoever looks round
Sees Eternity there.

JOHN CLARE / 1829

For I will consider my Cat Jeoffry.

For he is the servant of the Living God, duly and daily serving him.

For at the first glance of the glory of God in the East he worships in his way.

For this is done by wreathing his body seven times round with elegant quickness.

For then he leaps up to catch the musk, which is the blessing of God upon his prayer.

For he rolls upon prank to work it in.

For having done duty and received blessing he begins to consider himself.

For this he performs in ten degrees.

For first he looks upon his fore-paws to see if they are clean.

For secondly he kicks up behind to clear away there.

For thirdly he works it upon stretch with the fore-paws extended.

For fourthly he sharpens his paws by wood.

For fifthly he washes himself.

For sixthly he rolls upon wash.

For seventhly he fleas himself, that he may not be interrupted upon the beat.

For eighthly he rubs himself against a post.

For ninthly he looks up for his instructions.

For tenthly he goes in quest of food.

For having consider'd God and himself he will consider his neighbor. . . .

For he can catch the cork and toss it again.

For he is hated by the hypocrite and miser.

For the former is afraid of detection.

For the latter refuses the charge.

For he camels his back to bear the first notion of business.

For he is good to think on, if a man would express himself neatly.

For he made a great figure in Egypt for his signal services.
For he killed the Icneumon-rat very pernicious by land.
For his ears are so acute that they sting again.
For from this proceeds the passing quickness of his attention.
For by stroaking of him I have found out electricity.
For I perceived God's light about him both wax and fire.
For the Electrical fire is the spiritual substance, which God sends
    from heaven to sustain the bodies both of man and beast.
For God has blessed him in the variety of his movements.
For, tho' he cannot fly, he is an excellent clamberer.
For his motions upon the face of the earth are more than any
    other quadrupede.
For he can tread to all the measures upon the musick.
For he can swim for life.
For he can creep.

CHRISTOPHER SMART / 1763

> It seems a day
> (I speak of one from many singled out)
> One of those heavenly days that cannot die;
> When, in the eagerness of boyish hope,
> I left our cottage-threshold, sallying forth
> With a huge wallet o'ver my shoulders slung,
> A nutting-crook in hand; and turned my steps
> Tow'rd some far-distant wood, a Figure quaint,
> Tricked out in proud disguise of cast-off weeds
> Which for that service had been husbanded,
> By exhortation of my frugal Dame—
> Motley accoutrement, of power to smile
> At thorns, and brakes, and brambles,—and, in truth,
> More raggèd than need was! O'er pathless rocks,
> Through beds of matted fern, and tangled thickets,
> Forcing my way, I came to one dear nook
> Unvisited, where not a broken bough
> Drooped with its withered leaves, ungracious sign
> Of devastation; but the hazels rose
> Tall and erect, with tempting clusters hung,
> A virgin scene!—A little while I stood,
> Breathing with such suppression of the heart
> As joy delights in; and, with wise restraint
> Voluptuous, fearless of a rival, eyed
> The banquet;—or beneath the trees I sate
> Among the flowers, and with the flowers I played;
> A temper known to those, who, after long
> And weary expectation, have been blest
> With sudden happiness beyond all hope.
> Perhaps it was a bower beneath whose leaves
> The violets of five seasons re-appear
> And fade, unseen by any human eye;

Where fairy water-breaks do murmur on
For ever; and I saw the sparkling foam,
And—with my cheek on one of those green stones
That, fleeced with moss, under the shady trees,
Lay round me, scattered like a flock of sheep—
I heard the murmur and the murmuring sound,
In that sweet mood when pleasure loves to pay
Tribute to ease; and, of its joy secure,
The heart luxuriates with indifferent things,
Wasting its kindliness on stocks and stones,
And on the vacant air. Then up I rose,
And dragged to earth both branch and bough, with crash
And merciless ravage: and the shady nook
Of hazels, and the green and mossy bower,
Deformed and sullied, patiently gave up
Their quiet being: and, unless I now
Confound my present feelings with the past;
Ere from the mutilated bower I turned
Exulting, rich beyond the wealth of kings,
I felt a sense of pain when I beheld
The silent trees, and saw the intruding sky.—
Then, dearest Maiden, move along these shades
In gentleness of heart; with gentle hand
Touch—for there is a spirit in the woods.

WILLIAM WORDSWORTH / 1799

For I have learned
To look on nature, not as in the hour
Of thoughtless youth; but hearing oftentimes
The still, sad music of humanity,
Nor harsh nor grating, though of ample power
To chasten and subdue. And I have felt
A presence that disturbs me with the joy
Of elevated thoughts; a sense sublime
Of something far more deeply interfused,
Whose dwelling is the light of setting suns,
And the round ocean and the living air,
And the blue sky, and in the mind of man;
A motion and a spirit, that impels
All thinking things, all objects of all thought,
And rolls through all things.

WILLIAM WORDSWORTH / 1798

I

Season of mists and mellow fruitfulness.
  Close bosom-friend of the maturing sun;
Conspiring with him how to load and bless
  With fruit the vines that round the thatch-eves run;
To bend with apples the moss'd cottage-trees,
  And fill all fruit with ripeness to the core;
    To swell the gourd, and plump the hazel shells
  With a sweet kernel; to set budding more,
And still more, later flowers for the bees,
Until they think warm days will never cease,
    For Summer has o'er-brimm'd their clammy cells.

II

Who hath not seen thee oft amid thy store?
  Sometimes whoever seeks abroad may find
Thee sitting careless on a granary floor,
  Thy hair soft-lifted by the winnowing wind;
Or on a half-reap'd furrow sound asleep,
  Drows'd with the fume of poppies, while thy hook
    Spares the next swath and all its twined flowers:
And sometimes like a gleaner thou dost keep
  Steady thy laden head across a brook;
  Or by a cyder-press, with patient look,
    Thou watchest the last oozings hours by hours.

III

Where are the songs of Spring? Ay, where are they?
  Think not of them, thou hast thy music too,—
While barred clouds bloom the soft-dying day,
  And touch the stubble-plains with rosy hue;

Then in a wailful choir the small gnats mourn
   Among the river sallows, borne aloft
     Or sinking as the light wind lives or dies;
And full-grown lambs loud bleat from hilly bourn;
   Hedge-crickets sing; and now with treble soft
   The red-breast whistles from a garden-croft;
     And gathering swallows twitter in the skies.

JOHN KEATS / 1819

One summer evening (led by her) I found
A little boat tied to a willow tree
Within a rocky cove, its usual home.
Straight I unloosed her chain, and stepping in
Pushed from the shore. It was an act of stealth
And troubled pleasure, nor without the voice
Of mountain-echoes did my boat move on;
Leaving behind her still, on either side,
Small circles glittering idly in the moon,
Until they melted all into one track
Of sparkling light. But now, like one who rows,
Proud of his skill, to reach a chosen point
With an unswerving line, I fixed my view
Upon the summit of a craggy ridge,
The horizon's utmost boundary; far above
Was nothing but the stars and the grey sky.
She was an elfin pinnace; lustily
I dipped my oars into the silent lake,
And, as I rose upon the stroke, my boat
Went heaving through the water like a swan;
When, from behind that craggy steep till then
The horizon's bound, a huge peak, black and huge,
As if with voluntary power instinct,
Upreared its head. I struck and struck again,
And growing still in stature the grim shape
Towered up between me and the stars, and still,
For so it seemed, with purpose of its own
And measured motion like a living thing,
Strode after me. With trembling oars I turned,
And through the silent water stole my way
Back to the covert of the willow tree;
There in her mooring-place I left my bark,—

And through the meadows homeward went, in grave
And serious mood; but after I had seen
That spectacle, for many days, my brain
Worked with a dim and undetermined sense
Of unknown modes of being; o'er my thoughts
There hung a darkness, call it solitude
Or blank desertion. No familiar shapes
Remained, no pleasant images of trees,
Of sea or sky, no colours of green fields;
But huge and mighty forms, that do not live
Like living men, moved slowly through the mind
By day, and were a trouble to my dreams.

WILLIAM WORDSWORTH / 1798
from *The Prelude*

Who rides at night, who rides so late?
The father rides on, his child in his arms.
His arms are curled and firm round the boy,
He keeps him from falling, he keeps him warm.

"My boy, why is it you hide your face?"
"Dad, over there do you see the King?
The Invisible King with ermine and staff?"
"Dear boy, what you see is a rolling mist."

"*Hey there, my boy, come along with me!*
I have the neatest games you'll ever see.
On the shore my daisies blow in a line.
My mother has shirts all golden and fine."

"Dad, is it true you don't hear at all
The little gifts the King is offering me?"
"Calm down, my boy, no need for all this—
It's dry oak leaves making noise in the wind."

"*Child, good child, do you want to go?*
My daughters will care and wait on you so.
The great circle dance they do every night,
They'll sing and dance and tuck you in tight."

"Dad, it worries me that you don't see
The Daughters there at that ugly spot."
"I see the spot very clearly, my boy—
An old gray willow, that's all there is."

"*Your body is slim, and I love you.*
Come now, or seize you is what I'll do."
"Dad listen, please Dad, he's got hold of me!
He's done something bad to me, he has!"

The terrified father rides wilder and wilder;
The boy is now groaning as he sits slumped over;
In grief and fear at last the father got home.
The boy lay dead in the father's arms.

GOETHE / 1782
translated by Robert Bly

Have you been to that country where the gold
oranges and the lemony blossoms glow in dark leaves?
A soft wind winds down from the blue air,
The love myrtle rises quiet and Apollo's tree.
Have you been there? Truly? That is where
Oh my darling, I want to go with you!

Have you been to the Great House? Ionian columns
hold the roof, golden walls, rooms full of light,
Men of marble look at me without moving.
God help us, child, what have they done to you?
Have you been there? That is where,
Oh my Keeper from Harm, I want to go with you!

Have you been to the Mountain? Its stairs in cloud.
Hoofs of a mule pick their way through the fog.
Unconscious dragons breathe inside tunnels.
Granite splits, masses of water pour down.
Have you been there? That is where
the path we take goes! Oh my Father, it is time to go!

GOETHE / 1783
translated by Robert Bly

THE HOLY LONGING

Tell a wise person, or else keep silent,
because the massman will mock it right away.
I praise what is truly alive,
what longs to be burned to death.

In the calm water of the love-nights,
where you were begotten, where you have begotten,
a strange feeling comes over you
when you see the silent candle burning.

Now you are no longer caught
in the obsession with darkness,
and a desire for higher love-making
sweeps you upward.

Distance does not make you falter,
now, arriving in magic, flying,
and, finally, insane for the light,
you are the butterfly and you are gone.

And so long as you haven't experienced
this: to die and so to grow,
you are only a troubled guest
on the dark earth.

GOETHE / 1814
translated by Robert Bly

"HER FACE WAS IN A BED OF HAIR"

Her face was in a bed of hair,
Like flowers in a plot—
Her hand was whiter than the sperm
That feeds the sacred light.
Her tongue more tender than the tune
That totters in the leaves—
Who hears may be incredulous,
Who witnesses, believes.

EMILY DICKINSON / 1880?

71

The life in us is like the water in the river. It may rise this year higher than man has ever known it, and flood the parched uplands; even this may be the eventful year, which will drown out all our muskrats. It was not always dry land where we dwell. I see far inland the banks which the stream anciently washed, before science began to record its freshets. Every one has heard the story which has gone the rounds of New England, of a strong and beautiful bug which came out of the dry leaf of an old table of apple-tree wood, which had stood in a farmer's kitchen for sixty years, first in Connecticut, and afterward in Massachusetts,— from an egg deposited in the living tree many years earlier still, as appeared by counting the annual layers beyond it; which was heard gnawing out for several weeks, hatched perchance by the heat of an urn. Who does not feel his faith in a resurrection and immortality strengthened by hearing of this? Who knows what beautiful and winged life, whose egg has been buried for ages under many concentric layers of woodenness in the dead dry life of society, deposited at first in the alburnum of the green and living tree, which has been gradually converted into the semblance of its well-seasoned tomb,—heard perchance gnawing out now for years by the astonished family of man, as they sat round the festive board,—may unexpectedly come forth from amidst society's most trivial and handselled furniture, to enjoy its perfect summer life at last!

I do not say that John or Jonathan will realize all this; but such is the character of that morrow which mere lapse of time can never make to dawn. The light which puts out our eyes is darkness to us. Only that day dawns to which we are awake. There is more day to dawn. The sun is but a morning star.

HENRY DAVID THOREAU / 1854

Eva, I agree to love, among creation, all the creatures!
I will study them in your hypnotic eyes
From which the world receives so many shades,
Receives its elegant calm and spiritual mood:
Come, lay your cool hand on my ripped open heart,
But don't ever leave me alone with Nature,
For I know too much about her not to be afraid.

To me she says: "I am a theater that feels nothing;
The actor's feet can never move these boards;
My emerald flights of stairs, my alabaster halls,
My trunks of pure marble—the architect was divine.
Neither your sighs nor your cries reach my ears,
I hardly notice the humorous scenes humans make
As they search the sky for an audience not there.

"I let the human masses sail on without looking
At them or hearing them, as one does with ants;
I make no distinction between heaps and human ashes,
I give birth to nations but don't remember their names.
Humans say to me, "Mother," but I am a grave.
My winter accepts your corpses as a complimentary smoke,
My spring doesn't feel all your grateful feelings.

"Before you came, I was beautiful, my perfume elegant,
I shook my hair in all its masses to the wind,
I kept my old road through the spheres of the heavens,
Floating on the delicate harmony of the holy wheels.
When you're gone, cutting through space where all things go,
I will remain solitary and serene, pure and in silence,
I will part the air with my forehead and my glorious breasts."

Her voice so proud and sad spoke these things to me,
And far inside me what I feel is hate, and I see

73

Our blood in her ocean, and our corpses under her grasses,
Feeding the roots of the trees with their precious liquids.
And to my eyes that fell for her beauty, I say:
"Turn your looks elsewhere, turn all your tears away,
If you can see anything twice, it is not to be loved."

ALFRED DE VIGNY / 1844
translated by Robert Bly

I think I could turn and live with animals, they are so placid
   and self-contained,
I stand and look at them long and long.
They do not sweat and whine about their condition,
They do not lie awake in the dark and weep for their sins,
They do not make me sick discussing their duty to God,
Not one is dissatisfied, not one is demented with the mania of
   owning things,
Not one kneels to another, nor to his kind that lived thousands
   of years ago,
Not one is respectable or unhappy over the whole earth. . . .

A gigantic beauty of a stallion, fresh and responsive to my caresses,
Head high in the forehead, wide between the ears,
Limbs glossy and supple, tail dusting the ground,
Eyes full of sparkling wickedness, ears finely cut, flexibly moving.
His nostrils dilate as my heels embrace him,
His well-built limbs tremble with pleasure as we race around
   and return.

WALT WHITMAN / 1855

I live my life in growing orbits,
which move out over the things of the world.
Perhaps I can never achieve the last,
but that will be my attempt.

I am circling around God, around the ancient tower,
and I have been circling for a thousand years.
And I still don't know if I am a falcon,
Or a storm, or a great song.

RAINER MARIA RILKE / 1899
from *Book for the Hours of Prayer*
translated by Robert Bly

How shall I name you, immortal, mild, proud shadows?
I only know that all we know comes from you,
And that you come from Eden on flying feet.
Is Eden far away, or do you hide
From human thought, as hares and mice and coneys
That run before the reaping-hook and lie
In the last ridge of the barley? Do our woods
And winds and ponds cover more quiet woods,
More shining winds, more star-glimmering ponds?
Is Eden out of time and out of space?
And do you gather about us when pale light
Shining on water and fallen among leaves,
And winds blowing from flowers, and whirr of feathers
And the green quiet, have uplifted the heart?

I have made this poem for you, that men may read it
Before they read of Gorgael and Dectora,
As men in the old times, before the harps began,
Poured out wine for the high invisible ones.

W. B. YEATS / SEPTEMBER 1900
from *The Shadowy Waters*

Part three:
Poems of twofold consciousness, early twentieth century

What the poet is looking for
is not the fundamental I
but the deep you.

Antonio Machado
translated by Robert Bly

THE EARLY twentieth-century poets, especially the German and French, inherited a sweeping energy from the nineteenth century, a vigorous awareness of what language is like when it reaches outward to plants and metals, as well as inward to night-intelligence and sleep. Freud and Jung had one great advantage; in their twenties, they were able to read Goethe and Hölderlin, while the English doctors interested in psychology had only Matthew Arnold to read. Rainer Maria Rilke, whose work reaches an area of psychic abundance that many poets long for, had a similar advantage. He could read Hölderlin and Novalis early, and Freud and Jung later, in their associative originals.

I am suggesting that we have to reconsider what "modern" poetry is. It's true that a genuine tradition of modern poetry begins with the ironic and sarcastic poems of Corbière and La Forgue, and continues through Eliot, Auden, Cummings and Pound. We are aware of that tradition, and admire it. We are less aware of the Novalis–Hölderlin–Goethe tradition. Hölderlin, whose poems have such immense sound, reported that the new had come; but to him the new is not irony and dislocation, but the awareness that the old non-human or non-ego energies the ancient world imagined so well were impinging again on human consciousness. This tradition, which I consider to be the major one, had its source not in the era of 1885–1914, but earlier, in the German language of Novalis, the French of Gérard de Nerval, and the English of Blake. The mood of this tradition is not irony but swift association. Its aim is not to scant the modern world, but to approach the nourishment of night-intelligence.

Obviously this psychic longing is dangerous. Hitler, I think, perverted some magical intelligence to keep his power. Mankind's longing for night-intelligence, when adopted as a means to power, can transform itself quickly into Fascist rigidity. Ernst Becker describes how in *The Denial of Death*. Of course irony has its dark side too: Eliot's ironic intensity stood on reactionary Catholicism, which held up many Fascist buildings all over Europe. Pound's picaresque intensity rested on reactionary secularism; a few little Fascist huts stood there too. I believe the Novalis–Hölderlin–Goethe intensity, though also dangerous, is more sane. It stands on night-intelligence, the doctrine of many gods, and a firm respect for the ancient Greek and Celtic worlds.

The Christian Church, in its Augustinian emphasis on the evil of nature, from which human consciousness should out of sheer common sense hold itself aloof, contributed to the gap Western human beings feel between themselves and the universe. The Church, having done that, then had to comfort humans in the loneliness it helped to create. With a collective part of his personality, Eliot, in the "Love Song of J. Alfred Prufrock," expresses the obedient resignation as the Christian submits to the poverty of the Old Position:

> I have heard the mermaids singing each to each.
> I do not think that they will sing to me.

He says it in comedy, and yet with all the tragic implications of the resignation.

Rilke will not accept the psychic poverty that position implies, and he refuses to express Christian resignation; his suspicion of Christian virtue penetrates all his work. "Left out to die on the mountains of the heart" is his comment on the gap. He doesn't agree that the pagan gods are dead, and he imagines his conscious-

81

ness moving out steadily, in the way of orbits or rings, over "the things of the world." In "Leda" we experience a magnificent declaration of the union he thought still possible between divine and human consciousness. For that poem, he used personages drawn from the ancient world. Then in the *Sonnets to Orpheus* he restates his faith in open channels, this time in contemporary terms, in daily images he himself had experienced:

> Her sleep was everything.
> The trees I'd always loved, these distances that we
> can almost touch, the pastures I felt so much,
> and every miracle I found in myself.

This is the mood I miss most when reading Pound, or any of the ironic or satiric poets. Pound's work touches on the consciousness shared with animals at very few points. He looks obsessively in non-Western sources, China, for example, to find instances of resonant human life, but his pleasure at finding them could better be called, as Charles Upton has remarked, the despair of living in the gap.

In the German tradition, Boehme and the alchemists come before Goethe and Novalis, and Rilke comes after. In Spanish, the lineage includes Jiménez, Machado and Lorca, among others. Only one poet who wrote in English seems firmly in that tradition—Blake—but there are many individual poems that belong to it.

In North America, Robinson Jeffers, despite his freaky dislike of humans, sinks into something generous when he lays his hand intuitively on a rock, and Wallace Stevens is a genius many times over as, in "Anecdote of Men by the Thousand," he broods so affectionately over the influence landscape has on humans.

> The soul, he said, is composed
> Of the external world.
>
> There are men of the East, he said,
> Who are the East.
> There are men of a province
> Who are that province.

> There are men of a valley
> Who are that valley. . . .
>
> The mandoline is the instrument
> Of a place.
>
> Are there mandolines of western mountains?
> Are there mandolines of northern moonlight?
>
> The dress of a woman of Lhasa,
> In its place,
> Is an invisible element of that place
> Made visible.

Stevens and Frost, both geniuses, walk gingerly in this area just opened up, after being closed for centuries: the area where meeting a mandoline or a moose is meeting a consciousness. Frost's curious poem "The Most of It" becomes more suggestive when read alongside Hölderlin. He wanted a human response when he called out. Then he heard something crossing a small lake and he hoped it would be a human being, but it was an animal. It "forced the underbrush" and that was that. When a man and a woman in love stand looking at a stag and doe, it is not two people looking at animals, but "two look at two." Hart Crane's "Voyages II" leaps directly out of Blake. He says it will be the eyes of sexual lovers, which resemble the eyes of seals, that will at last see Paradise. And D. H. Lawrence we already know as a Blake disciple. His marvelous passage on whales mating goes this way:

> the long tip reaches strong, intense, like the maelstrom-tip,
>   and comes to rest
> in the clasp and the soft, wild clutch of a she-whale's fathomless body.
>
> And over the bridge of the whale's strong phallus, linking the wonder
>   of whales
> the burning archangels under the sea keep passing, back and forth.

His late poem, "Fish," which is too long to include here, has passages that equal the whale poem. After catching a pike, Lawrence says:

He was born in front of my sunrise,
Before my day.

He outstarts me.
And I, a many-fingered horror of daylight to him,
Have made him die.

Lorca carries into the twentieth century some of the medieval Arabic awareness of union and interfusion:

The rose
was not searching for darkness or science
borderline of flesh and dream,
it was searching for something else.

He grants consciousness, even the longing for higher consciousness, wholeheartedly, passionately, to olive groves and lizards; and his master, Juan Ramón Jiménez, began to brood at the end of his life over what "full consciousness" would be like, when people in the West finally achieved it. He says, talking to "full consciousness":

Here, in this third sea,
I can almost hear your voice: your voice, the wind,
filling entirely all movements . . .
marking out the roads with delight . . .

He described his own psyche late in life as

a black body
with a glowing diamond in its center.

This section covers roughly the years 1900–1945. It suggests poets one can read if one wants to see how this lineage of double consciousness or "full consciousness" appears in work currently available in English.

He thought he kept the universe alone;
For all the voice in answer he could wake
Was but the mocking echo of his own
From some tree-hidden cliff across the lake.
Some morning from the boulder-broken beach
He would cry out on life, that what it wants
Is not its own love back in copy speech,
But counter-love, original response.
And nothing ever came of what he cried
Unless it was the embodiment that crashed
In the cliff's talus on the other side,
And then in the far-distant water splashed,
But after a time allowed for it to swim,
Instead of proving human when it neared
And someone else additional to him,
As a great buck it powerfully appeared,
Pushing the crumpled water up ahead,
And landed pouring like a waterfall,
And stumbled through the rocks with horny tread,
And forced the underbrush—and that was all.

ROBERT FROST

SOMETIMES

Sometimes, when a bird cries out,
Or the wind sweeps through a tree,
Or a dog howls in a far off farm,
I hold still and listen a long time.

My soul turns and goes back to the place
Where, a thousand forgotten years ago,
The bird and the blowing wind
Were like me, and were my brothers.

My soul turns into a tree,
And an animal, and a cloud bank.
Then changed and odd it comes home
And asks me questions. What should I reply?

HERMANN HESSE
translated by Robert Bly

Love and forgetting might have carried them
A little further up the mountainside
With night so near, but not much further up.
They must have halted soon in any case
With thoughts of the path back, how rough it was
With rock and washout, and unsafe in darkness;
When they were halted by a tumbled wall
With barbed-wire binding. They stood facing this,
Spending what onward impulse they still had
In one last look the way they must not go,
On up the failing path, where, if a stone
Or earthslide moved at night, it moved itself;
No footstep moved it. "This is all," they sighed,
"Good-night to woods." But not so; there was more.
A doe from round a spruce stood looking at them
Across the wall, as near the wall as they.
She saw them in their field, they her in hers.
The difficulty of seeing what stood still,
Like some up-ended boulder split in two,
Was in her clouded eyes: they saw no fear there.
She seemed to think that, two thus, they were safe.
Then, as if they were something that, though strange,
She could not trouble her mind with too long,
She sighed and passed unscared along the wall.
"*This*, then, is all. What more is there to ask?"
But no, not yet. A snort to bid them wait.
A buck from round the spruce stood looking at them
Across the wall, as near the wall as they.
This was an antlered buck of lusty nostril,
Not the same doe come back into her place.
He viewed them quizzically with jerks of head,
As if to ask, "Why don't you make some motion?

Or give some sign of life? Because you can't.
I doubt if you're as living as you look."
Thus till he had them almost feeling dared
To stretch a proffering hand—and a spell-breaking.
Then he too passed unscared along the wall.
Two had seen two, whichever side you spoke from.
"This *must* be all." It was all. Still they stood,
A great wave from it going over them,
As if the earth in one unlooked-for favor
Had made them certain earth returned their love.

ROBERT FROST

My long two-pointed ladder's sticking through a tree
Toward heaven still,
And there's a barrel that I didn't fill
Beside it, and there may be two or three
Apples I didn't pick upon some bough.
But I am done with apple-picking now.
Essence of winter sleep is on the night,
The scent of apples: I am drowsing off.
I cannot rub the strangeness from my sight
I got from looking through a pane of glass
I skimmed this morning from the drinking trough
And held against the world of hoary grass.
It melted, and I let it fall and break.
But I was well
Upon my way to sleep before it fell,
And I could tell
What form my dreaming was about to take.
Magnified apples appear and disappear,
Stem end and blossom end,
And every fleck of russet showing clear.
My instep arch not only keeps the ache,
It keeps the pressure of a ladder-round.
I feel the ladder sway as the boughs bend.
And I keep hearing from the cellar bin
The rumbling sound
Of load on load of apples coming in.
For I have had too much
Of apple-picking: I am overtired
Of the great harvest I myself desired.
There were ten thousand thousand fruit to touch,
Cherish in hand, lift down, and not let fall.
For all

That struck the earth,
No matter if not bruised or spiked with stubble,
Went surely to the cider-apple heap
As of no worth.
One can see what will trouble
This sleep of mine, whatever sleep it is.
Were he not gone,
The woodchuck could say whether it's like his
Long sleep, as I describe its coming on,
Or just some human sleep.

ROBERT FROST

90

A pale morning in June 4 AM
the country roads still greyish and moist
tunnelling endlessly through pines
a car had passed by on the dusty road
where an ant was out with his pine needle working
he was wandering around in the huge F of Firestone
that had been pressed into the sandy earth
for a hundred and twenty kilometers.
Fir needles are heavy.
Time after time he slipped back with his badly balanced
load
and worked it up again
and skidded back again
travelling over the great and luminous Sahara lit by clouds.

ROLF JACOBSEN
translated by Robert Bly

SUNFLOWER

What sower walked over earth,
which hands sowed
our inward seeds of fire?
They went out from his fists like rainbow curves
to frozen earth, young loam, hot sand,
they will sleep there
greedily, and drink up our lives
and explode it into pieces
for the sake of a sunflower that you haven't seen
or a thistle head or a chrysanthemum.

Let the young rain of tears come.
Let the calm hands of grief come.
It's not all as evil as you think.

ROLF JACOBSEN
translated by Robert Bly

ROAD'S END

The roads have come to their end now,
they don't go any farther, they turn here,
over on the earth there.
You can't go any farther if you don't want
to go to the moon or the planets. Stop now
in time, and turn to a wasp's nest or a cow track,
a volcano opening or a clatter of stones in the woods—
it's all the same. Something else.

They won't go any farther as I've said
without changing, the engine to horseshoes,
the gear shift to a fir branch
    which you hold loose in your hand
—what the hell is this?   indeed

ROLF JACOBSEN
translated by Robert Bly

THE FIRST PSALM

1. The convex face of the black countries is so terrifying in
the night! *The round face in the forest is so terrifying
in the night*

2. Above the world there's the clouds, they're part of the
world. Above the clouds—nothing.

3. The tree all alone in the stony field must have the *SENSE* sensation
that it's all pointless. He has never even seen a *another* tree. There are
no trees. *(other selves)*

4. The thought *HAUNTS* comes to me all the time: we are not being
watched. Exile of a single star in the night, before it goes down!

5. The warm wind is extremely interested in everything being
connected, he's a Catholic.

6. You don't find people like me very often. I don't have any
patience. Our old brother That's All said of the earth: it isn't
doing a thing!

7. We are travelling with tremendous speed toward a star in
the Milky Way. A great repose is visible on the face of the
earth. My heart's a little fast. Otherwise everything's fine.

BERTOLT BRECHT
translated by Robert Bly

94

Trundled from
the strangeness of the sea—
a kind of
heaven—

Ladies and Gentlemen!
the greatest
sea-monster ever exhibited
alive

the gigantic
sea-elephant! O wallow
of flesh where
are

there fish enough for
that
appetite stupidity
cannot lessen?

Sick
of April's smallness
the little
leaves—

Flesh has lief of you
enormous sea—
Speak!
Blouaugh! (feed

me) my
flesh is riven—
fish after fish into his maw
unswallowing

to let them glide down
gulching back
half spittle half
brine

the
troubled eyes—torn
from the sea.
(In

a practical voice) They
ought
to put it back where
it came from.

Gape.
Strange head—
told by old sailors—
rising

bearded
to the surface—and
the only
sense out of them

is that woman's
Yes
it's wonderful but they
ought to

put it
back into the sea where
it came from.
Blouaugh!

Swing—ride
walk

on wires—toss balls
stoop and

contort yourselves—
But I
am love. I am
from the sea—

Blouaugh!
there is no crime save
the too-heavy
body

the sea
held playfully—comes
to the surface
the water

boiling
about the head the cows
scattering
fish dripping from

the bounty
of . . . . and spring
they say
Spring is icummen in—

WILLIAM CARLOS WILLIAMS

They say the sea is cold, but the sea contains
the hottest blood of all, and the wildest, the most urgent.

All the whales in the wider deeps, hot are they, as they urge
on and on, and dive beneath the icebergs.
The right whales, the sperm-whales, the hammer-heads, the
    killers
there they blow, there they blow, hot wild white breath out
    of the sea!

And they rock, and they rock, through the sensual ageless ages
on the depths of the seven seas,
and through the salt they reel with drunk delight
and in the tropics tremble they with love
and roll with massive, strong desire, like gods.
Then the great bull lies up against his bride
in the blue deep bed of the sea,
as mountain pressing on mountain, in the zest of life:
and out of the inward roaring of the inner red ocean of
    whale-blood
the long tip reaches strong, intense, like the maelstrom-tip, and
    comes to rest
in the clasp and the soft, wild clutch of a she-whale's
    fathomless body.

And over the bridge of the whale's strong phallus, linking the
    wonder of whales
the burning archangels under the sea keep passing, back and forth,
keep passing, archangels of bliss
from him to her, from her to him, great Cherubim
that wait on whales in mid-ocean, suspended in the waves of
    the sea
great heaven of whales in the waters, old hierarchies.

And enormous mother whales lie dreaming suckling their
    whale-tender young
and dreaming with strange whale eyes wide open in the waters
    of the beginning and the end.

And bull-whales gather their women and whale-calves in a ring
when danger threatens, on the surface of the ceaseless flood
and range themselves like great fierce Seraphim facing the threat
encircling their huddled monsters of love.
And all this happens in the sea, in the salt
where God is also love, but without words:
and Aphrodite is the wife of whales
most happy, happy she!

and Venus among the fishes skips and is a she-dolphin
she is the gay, delighted porpoise sporting with love and the sea
she is the female tunny-fish, round and happy among the males
and dense with happy blood, dark rainbow bliss in the sea.

D. H. LAWRENCE

Man, introverted man, having crossed
In passage and but a little with the nature of things this
    latter century
Has begot giants; but being taken up
Like a maniac with self-love and inward conflicts cannot manage
    his hybrids.
Being used to deal with edgeless dreams,
Now he's bred knives on nature turns them also inward:
    they have thirsty points though.
His mind forebodes his own destruction;
Actæon who saw the goddess naked among leaves and his
    hounds tore him.
A little knowledge, a pebble from the shingle,
A drop from the oceans: who would have dreamed this
    infinitely little too much?

ROBINSON JEFFERS

ANIMALS

At dawn a knot of sea-lions lies off the shore
In the slow swell between the rock and the cliff,
Sharp flippers lifted, or great-eyed heads, as they roll in the sea,
Bigger than draft-horses, and barking like dogs
Their all-night song. It makes me wonder a little
That life near kin to human, intelligent, hot-blooded, idle and
    singing, can float at ease
In the ice-cold midwinter water. Then, yellow dawn
Colors the south, I think about the rapid and furious lives
    in the sun:
They have little to do with ours; they have nothing to do with
    oxygen and salted water; they would look monstrous
If we could see them: the beautiful passionate bodies of living
    flame, batlike flapping and screaming,
Tortured with burning lust and acute awareness, that ride the
    storm-tides
Of the great fire-globe. They are animals, as we are. There are
    many other chemistries of animal life
Besides the slow oxidation of carbohydrates and amino-acids.

ROBINSON JEFFERS

OH, LOVELY ROCK

We stayed the night in the pathless gorge of Ventana Creek, up
    the east fork.
The rock walls and the mountain ridges hung forest on forest
    above our heads, maple and redwood,
Laurel, oak, madrone, up to the high and slender Santa Lucian
    firs that stare up the cataracts
Of slide-rock to the star-color precipices.

                We lay on gravel and kept a little camp-fire
    for warmth.
Past midnight only two or three coals glowed red in the cooling
    darkness; I laid a clutch of dead bay-leaves
On the ember ends and felted dry sticks across them and lay
    down again. The revived flame
Lighted my sleeping son's face and his companion's, and the
    vertical face of the great gorge-wall
Across the stream. Light leaves overhead danced in the fire's
    breath, tree-trunks were seen: it was the rock wall
That fascinated my eyes and mind. Nothing strange: light-gray
    diorite with two or three slanting seams in it,
Smooth-polished by the endless attrition of slides and floods; no
    fern nor lichen, pure naked rock . . . as if I were
Seeing rock for the first time. As if I were seeing through the
    flame-lit surface into the real and bodily
And living rock. Nothing strange . . . I cannot
Tell you how strange: the silent passion, the deep nobility and
    childlike loveliness: this fate going on
Outside our fates. It is here in the mountain like a grave
    smiling child. I shall die, and my boys
Will live and die, our world will go on through its rapid
    agonies of change and discovery; this age will die,

And wolves have howled in the snow around a new Bethlehem:
    this rock will be here, grave, earnest, not passive: the energies
That are its atoms will still be bearing the whole mountain
    above: and I, many packed centuries ago,
Felt its intense reality with love and wonder, this lonely rock.

ROBINSON JEFFERS

—And yet this great wink of eternity,
Of rimless floods, unfettered leewardings,
Samite sheeted and processioned where
Her undinal vast belly moonward blends,
Laughing the wrapt inflections of our love;

Take this Sea, whose diapason knells
On scrolls of silver snowy sentences,
The sceptred terror of whose sessions rends
As her demeanors motion well or ill,
All but the pieties of lovers' hands.

And onward, as bells off San Salvador
Salute the crocus lustres of the stars,
In these poinsettia meadows of her tides,—
Adagios of islands, O my Prodigal,
Complete the dark confessions her veins spell.

Mark how her turning shoulders wind the hours,
And hasten while her penniless rich palms
Pass superscription of bent foam and wave,—
Hasten, while they are true,—sleep, death, desire,
Close round one instant in one floating flower.

Bind us in time, O Seasons clear, and awe.
O minstrel galleons of Carib fire,
Bequeath us to no earthly shore until
Is answered in the vortex of our grave
The seal's wide spindrift gaze toward paradise.

HART CRANE

OCEANS

   I have a feeling that my boat
has struck, down there in the depths,
against a great thing.
                 And nothing
happens! Nothing . . . Silence . . . Waves . . .

   —Nothing happens? Or has everything happened,
and are we standing now, quietly, in the new life?

JUAN RAMÓN JIMÉNEZ
translated by Robert Bly

The lamb was bleating softly.
The young jackass grew happier
with his excited bray.
The dog barked,
almost talking to the stars.
    I woke up! I went out. I saw the tracks
of the sky on the ground
which had flowered
like a sky
turned upside down.
    A warm and mild haze
hung around the trees;
the moon was going down
in a west of gold and silk
like some full and divine womb . . .
    My chest was thumping
as if my heart were drunk . . .
    I opened the barn door to see if
He was there.
                He was!

JUAN RAMÓN JIMÉNEZ
translated by Robert Bly

FULL CONSCIOUSNESS

You are carrying me, full consciousness, god that has desires,
all through the world.
                              Here, in this third sea,
I almost hear your voice: your voice, the wind,
filling entirely all movements;
eternal colors and eternal lights,
sea colors and sea lights.

Your voice of white fire
in the universe of water, the ship, the sky,
marking out the roads with delight,
engraving for me with a blazing light my firm orbit:
a black body
with the glowing diamond in its center.

JUAN RAMÓN JIMÉNEZ
translated by Robert Bly

Corridors of the soul! The soul that is like a young woman!
You clear light
and the brief history
and the joy of a new life . . .

Oh turn and be born again, and walk the road,
and find once more the lost path!

And turn and feel in our own hand
the warmth of the good hand
of our mother . . . And walk through life in dreams
out of love of the hand that leads us.

⏣ ⏣ ⏣

In our soul everything
moves guided by a mysterious hand:
ununderstandable, not speaking,
we know nothing of our own souls.

The deepest words
of the wise men teach us
the same as the whistle of the wind when it blows,
or the sound of the water when it is flowing.

ANTONIO MACHADO
translated by Robert Bly

The rose
was not searching for the sunrise:
almost eternal on its branch,
it was searching for something else.

The rose
was not searching for darkness or science:
borderline of flesh and dream,
it was searching for something else.

The rose
was not searching for the rose.
Motionless in the sky
it was searching for something else.

FEDERICO GARCÍA LORCA
translated by Robert Bly

(*Office and Attack*)

·To Fernando Vela

    Beneath all the statistics
there is a drop of duck's blood.
Beneath all the columns
there is a drop of a sailor's blood.
Beneath all the totals, a river of warm blood;
a river that goes singing
past the bedrooms of the suburbs,
and the river is silver, cement, or wind
in the lying daybreak of New York
The mountains exist, I know that.
And the lenses ground for wisdom,
I know that. But I have not come to see the sky.
I have come to see the stormy blood,
the blood that sweeps the machines to the waterfalls,
and the spirit on to the cobra's tongue.
Every day they kill in New York
ducks, four million,
pigs, five million,
pigeons, two thousand, for the enjoyment of dying men,
cows, one million,
lambs, one million,
roosters, two million
who turn the sky to small splinters.
You may as well sob filing a razor blade
or assassinate dogs in the hallucinated foxhunts,
as try to stop in the dawnlight
the endless trains carrying milk,
the endless trains carrying blood,
and the trains carrying roses in chains
for those in the field of perfume.

The ducks and the pigeons
and the hogs and the lambs
lay their drops of blood down
underneath all the statistics;
and the terrible bawling of the packed-in cattle
fills the valley with suffering
where the Hudson is getting drunk on its oil.
I attack all those persons
who know nothing of the other half,
the half who cannot be saved,
who raise their cement mountains
in which the hearts of the small
animals no one thinks of are beating,
and from which we will all fall
during the final holiday of the drills.
I spit in your face.
The other half hears me,
as they go on eating, urinating, flying in their purity
like the children of the janitors
who carry delicate sticks
to the holes where the antennas
of the insects are rusting.
This is not hell, it is a street.
This is not death, it is a fruit-stand.
There is a whole world of crushed rivers and unachievable
      distances
in the paw of a cat crushed by a car,
and I hear the song of the worm
in the heart of so many girls.
Rust, rotting, trembling earth.
And you are earth, swimming through the figures of the office.
What shall I do, set my landscape in order?
Set in place the lovers who will afterwards be photographs,
who will be bits of wood and mouthfuls of blood?
No, I won't; I attack,

I attack the conspiring
of these empty offices
that will not broadcast the sufferings,
that rub out the plans of the forest,
and I offer myself to be eaten by the packed-up cattle
when their mooing fills the valley
where the Hudson is getting drunk on its oil.

FEDERICO GARCÍA LORCA
translated by Robert Bly

ENIGMAS

You've asked me what the lobster is weaving there with his
    golden feet?
I reply, the ocean knows this.
You say, what is the ascidia waiting for in its transparent bell?
    What is it waiting for?
I tell you it is waiting for time, like you.
You ask me whom the Macrocystis alga hugs in its arms?
Study, study it, at a certain hour, in a certain sea I know.
You question me about the wicked tusk of the narwhal, and I
    reply by describing
how the sea unicorn with the harpoon in it dies.
You enquire about the kingfisher's feathers,
which tremble in the pure springs of the southern tides?
Or you've found in the cards a new question touching on the
    crystal architecture
of the sea anemone, and you'll deal that to me now?
You want to understand the electric nature of the ocean spines?
    The armored stalactite that breaks as it walks?
    The hook of the angler fish, the music stretched out in the
        deep places like a thread in the water?

    I want to tell you the ocean knows this, that life in its
        jewel boxes
is endless as the sand, impossible to count, pure,
and among the blood-colored grapes time has made the petal
hard and shiny, made the jellyfish full of light
and untied its knot, letting its musical threads fall
from a horn of plenty made of infinite mother-of-pearl.

    I am nothing but the empty net which has gone on ahead
of human eyes, dead in those darknesses,
of fingers accustomed to the triangle, longitudes
on the timid globe of an orange.

113

I walked around as you do, investigating
the endless star,
and in my net, during the night, I woke up naked,
the only thing caught, a fish trapped inside the wind.

PABLO NERUDA
translated by Robert Bly

One must have a mind of winter
To regard the frost and the boughs
Of the pine-trees crusted with snow;

And have been cold a long time
To behold the junipers shagged with ice,
The spruces rough in the distant glitter

Of the January sun; and not to think
Of any misery in the sound of the wind,
In the sound of a few leaves,

Which is the sound of the land
Full of the same wind
That is blowing in the same bare place

For the listener, who listens in the snow,
And, nothing himself, beholds
Nothing that is not there and the nothing that is.

WALLACE STEVENS

It was when I said,
"There is no such thing as the truth,"
That the grapes seemed fatter.
The fox ran out of his hole.

You . . . You said,
"There are many truths,
But they are not parts of a truth."
Then the tree, at night, began to change,

Smoking through green and smoking blue.
We were two figures in a wood.
We said we stood alone.

It was when I said,
"Words are not forms of a single word.
In the sum of the parts, there are only the parts.
The world must be measured by eye";

It was when you said,
"The idols have seen lots of poverty,
Snakes and gold and lice,
But not the truth";

It was at that time, that the silence was largest
And longest, the night was roundest,
The fragrance of the autumn warmest,
Closest and strongest.

WALLACE STEVENS

So earth's inclined toward the one invisible,
The prince of space, and yet he was disproved,
But this is her nuptial night, a cruel season
As limbless lizards coil together in love

And her whiteness veils over the dog-faced owl,
Whiteness veils over the frozen streams, the moon,
And the deer islanded without family,
Nuzzling cold tulips. Whiteness veils over the sea,

And the heart of the snail is beating slow.
But as an early bride, with heaven's rose
She is adorned, she is wound in seven veils
Even as a bride going forth to the bridegroom,

And her whiteness veils over the scarred fields.
She is celebrant for the failure of a theory,
And the white ptarmigan treads in the snow among the low hills.

MARGUERITE YOUNG

When the god, needing something, decided to become a swan,
he was astounded how lovely the bird was;
he was dizzy as he disappeared into the swan.
But his deceiving soon pulled him into the doing,

before he had a chance to test all the new feelings
inside the being. And the woman, open to him,
recognized the One Soon To Be in the swan
and she knew: what he asked for

was something which, confused in her defending, she
could no longer keep from him. He pressed closer
and pushing his neck through her less and less firm hand

let the God loose into the heavenly woman.
Then for the first time he found his feathers marvellous
and lying in her soft place he became a swan.

RAINER MARIA RILKE
translated by Robert Bly

The kings of the world are growing old,
and they shall have no inheritors.
Their sons died while they were boys,
and their neurasthenic daughters abandoned
the sick crown to the mob.

The mob breaks it into tiny bits of gold.
The Lord of the World, master of the age,
melts them in fire into machines,
which do his orders with low growls;
but luck is not on their side.

The ore feels homesick. It wants to abandon
the minting houses and the wheels
that offer it such a meager life.
And out of factories and payroll boxes
it wants to go back into the veins
of the thrown-open mountain,
which will close again behind it.

RAINER MARIA RILKE
translated by Robert Bly

MOVING AHEAD

Once more my deeper life goes on with more strength,
as if the banks through which it moves had widened out.
Trees and stones seem more like me each day,
and the paintings I see seem more seen into:
with my senses, as with the birds, I climb
into the windy heaven out of the oak,
and in the ponds broken off from the blue sky
my feeling sinks, as if standing on fishes.

RAINER MARIA RILKE
translated by Robert Bly

I can tell by the way the trees beat, after
so many dull days, on my worried windowpanes,
that a storm is coming,
and I hear the far-off fields say things
I can't bear without a friend,
I can't love without a sister.

The storm, the shifter of shapes, drives on
across the woods and across time,
and the world looks as if it had no age:
the landscape, like a line in the psalm book,
is seriousness and weight and eternity.

What we choose to fight is so tiny!
What fights with us is so great!
If only we would let ourselves be dominated
as things do by some immense storm,
we would become strong too, and not need names.

When we win it's with small things,
and the triumph itself makes us small.
What is extraordinary and eternal
does not *want* to be bent by us.
I mean the angel, who appeared
to the wrestlers of the Old Testament:
when the wrestler's sinews
grew long like metal strings,
he felt them under his fingers
like chords of deep music.

Whoever was beaten by this Angel,
(who often simply declined the fight),
went away proud and strengthened

and great from that harsh hand,
that kneaded him as if to change his shape.
Winning does not tempt that man.
This is how he grows: by being defeated, decisively,
by constantly greater beings.

RAINER MARIA RILKE
translated by Robert Bly

Part four:
Poems of twofold consciousness,
1945-1979

I should be content
to look at a mountain
for what it is
and not as a comment
on my life.

David Ignatow

I n his book, *Flight from Woman*, Karl Stern retells the three dreams Descartes dreamed the night before his formulation took its final shape. Descartes was about to settle on this division: the world is made of a *res cogitans*, which Stern rephrases as a "think-ing something" that has no spatial quality, and a *res extensa*, a "spatial something" that has no psychic quality. Descartes in his first dream found himself trying to walk in a powerful wind, and as he walked he was bent over strongly to his left—that is to say, physically his left side became scrunched down, compressed, or crushed. He was surprised to see other people walking upright in the same wind. This dream is especially suggestive when we con-sider the recent speculation, reported by Robert Ornstein in *The Psychology of Consciousness*, that the two halves of the body respond to and embody the modes of the opposite brain lobe. Space apparently locates itself in the left side of the body. The left side also favors feeling, music, motion, touch, in brief, the qualities in us that enable us to unite with objects and creatures. The right side of the body favors the qualities we use to separate us from objects, in order to get the distance necessary for analysis; those include abstract language, concept, measurement of time, restraint of emotion, the study of ethics, law.

We are all bent over now, walking like Descartes, our left side crushed. Our feelings lack air, the space has been pressed out. As Rilke said, "Everywhere I am folded, there I am a lie." So Descartes' first dream seems to have been a sort of prediction of what would happen, not only to himself, but to the entire society.

Descartes woke from this dream, wrote it down, and tried to interpret it "according to his philosophy." He then fell asleep and this time saw fiery sparks floating in the room. After this second dream he got to sleep with difficulty.

In his third dream some terrifying things happened. A book disappeared from his hand. A book appeared at one end of his table, vanished, and appeared at the other end. And the dictionary, when he checked it, had fewer words in it than it had a few minutes before. I suspect that we are losing some words that inhabit the left side; our vocabulary is getting smaller. The disappearing words are probably words such as "mole," "ocean," "praise," "whale," "steeping," "bat-ear," "wooden tub," "moist cave," "seawind."

So one could say that the whole Novalis–Hölderlin–Goethe tradition I've spoken of is an attempt to reclaim for the psyche certain disappearing words, thereby preventing the reality behind them from disappearing into amnesia. The words have to be looked for, since they are hidden in the folds of the bent-over left side. We could say, then, that the poetry of the last hundred years— of all schools—is an effort to unfold the left side of the body. Eliot's contribution there has been tremendous, so has Williams' and the work of the younger poets. Freud and Jung, by taking steps backward, into the ancient past, have achieved an unfolding very moving to watch; the archeology of Schliemann and Wooley and others have brought much left-side material up. That work goes on. But the situation is complicated. Our left side continues to unfold steadily, and yet in each decade a new form of folding takes place. One sometimes meets nuclear power advocates with almost no left side at all. I feel that in all of us the left side remains heavily folded, and this is true of women and men. Yet the longing for the left side to unfold, the thirst for the space of feeling, grows. Machado said:

> It is good knowing that glasses
> are to drink from;
> the bad thing is not to know
> what thirst is for.

My job in this section is to trace what I have called the Novalis–Hölderlin–Goethe tradition on through the poems written by poets here and abroad in the years since 1945. It has not been the dominant tradition during those years in the United States. I think war crushes the unfolding left side all over again, and the dominant tradition since World War II has been the human-obsessed art of Norman Mailer and Roth and the confessionalism of Robert Lowell. By "life studies," Lowell really means a study of himself, not of pears or apples, which is what the French painters meant by the phrase. The movement didn't turn out well for Plath or Sexton, who both ended as suicides. One suicide was associated with an oven, the other with the poet's mother's old coat; and I think that these details mean that confessional poetry traps women precisely where they don't want to be, in the domestic. By concentrating on anger they lose their thirst for mountains. The investigation of the anger is important, and yet the work of confessional poets is remarkable for the absence of tree-detail or praise of landscape. Berryman's work likewise becomes concentrated on the human; he too dies a suicide. Many American editors show no awareness whatever of the Novalis–Hölderlin–Goethe stream, nor the praising tradition of Rilke; and they sometimes have to import reviewers from England to find writers capable of concentrating exclusively on the human. England still keeps the Old Position supported in the manner to which it is accustomed.

When a country wins a war, the victory increases the arrogance of its writers, and I feel we are still suffering the results of the victory of 1945. The American writers who take European masters are fewer than in the Twenties. Antonio Machado remarks

> *This modern narcissist of ours*
> *cannot see his face in the mirror*
> *because he has become the mirror.*

Narcissism is an elegant form of the Old Position, and the whole culture of the Seventies shows wide traces of it. Machado suggests that narcissism has taken a step beyond the well-known dandyism of the nineteenth century. The outer world now no longer provides a mirror for the human being to see himself in; instead, the human being puts himself out there, and replaces nature with his own body or his "consciousness."

The Novalis–Hölderlin–Goethe tradition, then, embodies a struggle against narcissism. One notices that in such poetry the serene or transparent style becomes useful, and one notices that attention to sound is important. It is possible that the poem in this tradition becomes serene on the surface in order that it may become transparent. The poet does not insist on presenting all the events of his life, and doesn't refuse to present them either. He brings in enough to make the poem his, but is sparing, so that space opens behind the details, just as there is space between stars in a constellation, so that through the space the reader may see the outer world, may see the mountain night. Anna Akhmatova is a master of this sparing use of personal detail. The poems clearly come from her "life," and yet through them we glimpse something else, not "hers."

> *Sand on the bottom whiter than chalk,*
> *and the air drunk, like wine;*
> *late sun lays bare*
> *the rosy limbs of the pinetrees.*
>
> *Sunset in the ethereal waves:*
> *I cannot tell if the day*
> *is ending, or the world, or if*
> *the secret of secrets is inside me again.*

In the poetry of twofold consciousness, the Novalis–Hölderlin–Goethe stream, the poets of the West Coast have done better on the whole than the poets of the East Coast in recent decades. I think it is because there have been better teachers in the West. Denise Levertov remains in the East, but her work has many early roots in the ground that Kenneth Rexroth prepared. Rexroth's *The Signature of All Things* is surely one of the greatest of all American books, and rich influence from that book is also evident in Gary Snyder, Robert Creeley and James Wright. Gary Snyder's language is "riprapped" for clarity, and his praise of the outward world consistent and persistent. Snyder's work—"This Poem Is for Bear" is an example—hints continually of the interplay between humans and animals in their consciousness. I first read Antonio Machado in Rexroth's translation, and my first book, *Silence in the Snowy Fields*, is much indebted to Machado and to Rexroth. Robinson Jeffers and his fierce student, William Everson (or Brother Antoninus), have taught certain attitudes and intensities that no one in the East has stood for; William Stafford considers himself a disciple of Jeffers. Theodore Roethke in Seattle taught magnificently even in the classrooms; Robert Sund and James Wright are among his students.

Denise Levertov's language—calm, decisive, clear in sound, energetic—often becomes marvelously transparent:

> Cold of the sea is counterpart
> to the great fire. Plunging
> out of the burning cold of ocean
> we enter an ocean of intense
> noon. Sacred salt
> sparkles on our bodies.
>
> After mist has wrapped us again
> in fine wool, may the taste of salt
> recall to us the great depths about us.

Robert Duncan, firmly rooted in the West, grows also from some ground prepared partly by Rexroth. The body of his work approaches some area that is not exactly Christian, nor secular, nor mental, nor physical, but an area more connected with transformation of bodies. He writes of the Lady:

She it is Queen Under The Hill
whose hosts are a disturbance of words within words
that is a field folded.

It is only a dream of the grass blowing
east against the source of the sun
in an hour before the sun's going down

whose secret we see in a children's game
of ring a round of roses told.

Often I am permitted to return to a meadow
as if it were a given property of the mind
that certain bounds hold against chaos,

that is a place of first permission,
everlasting omen of what is.

The United States has produced its first Alaskan poet. John Haines took up a homestead in Alaska around 1954, and remained there fifteen years. His *Winter News* and later books of poems contain several masterpieces of the transparent poem. A genuine sense of the Alaskan landscape is present.

The gradual unfolding of the left side in poetry since 1945 has been aided by several new developments. For one thing, the concept of the shaman has entered, for the first time in the history of poetry in English. This step was the fruit of labor by anthropologists and their enthusiasm for primitive cultures, and is associated in poetry with Gary Snyder, Jerome Rothenberg and others. It's a dangerous addition, because if the poet takes it as a fashion, it becomes a way to separate himself from the human community; he simply lives nostalgically, in barren archetypes. But the Eskimo shaman takes on illnesses, visits other worlds, reminds each person he or she meets of the night side, belongs to no class. Poets in Europe and America, not knowing how to imagine themselves, often have ended as moral spokesmen for their own class or an adopted one. Pope is an example, also Kerouac. The shaman concept gives other alternatives beyond the silly division of poets into "academic" or "beat," "cooked" or "raw." He is neither cooked nor raw. The concept also gives the poet a tunnel back into the far human past. In some manner, the shaman concept is also connected to doing physical work. Moreover, the shaman works in the spiritual world, but not as a part of high culture. The Taoist stream in China, which has nourished, strenghtened and deepened the ancient Chinese poet so much, may be considered as a cunning continuation of shamanism into post-tribal circumstances. On the other hand, the exploitation by some poets of American Indian religion seems to me disgusting.

In another, related development, American poetry has finally begun to draw on the mood of the ancient Chinese poem. Perhaps the greatest obstacle that faces a poet who is trying to develop the transparent poem is the fascinating power of the rhetorical style. We take in the style through Milton and Donne, so pervasively studied in school, and through American poets such as Whittier. It is the sort of style teachers like, touched with obvious craft. The example of ancient Chinese poetry, originally introduced by Arthur Waley, and continued lately by Robert Payne and others, has suggested to recent American poets that to be a poet may not mean throwing yourself like an enormous wave up a cliff, raging against Heaven, as Milton did, but may instead mean flowing quietly, almost transparently, as water flows over grass. This possibility comes as a surprise, usually, to the person trained in the rhetorical style; the surprise is beautifully captured in a story about an imaginary character developed by the Sufis named Mullah Nasrudin, around whom various teaching stories gathered. It seems Mullah had always lived inland, and one day, when he was thirty or so, visited the sea for the first time. The wind is high; he is astonished, waves come smashing on the rocks, the noise is strong, foam flies around, water explodes. Mullah then kneels down to taste it, and says, "Amazing! That something so pretentious should be undrinkable!"

For a poem to be drinkable does not mean it has to be written in free verse, or as a prose poem. The Chinese, after several hundred years of "free verse" developed by attention to sound and pitch a form that is transparent in the way rhyme and meter are not. I am not making a principle here, that iambic meter and rhyme are always rhetorical; Richard Wilbur often manages to be beautifully transparent using English meter and rhyme. I'm talking only of degrees, and the possibility of developing a new form based on sound and pitch. We can sense a new concept of form floating delicately under John Logan's long-time study of sound.

> Well, what then?
> The one old and the two young
> men. Two fresh stones, or wells—
> and the powerful, untried pen.

A third advance I see is the massive movement of poetry toward recitation, toward words that float in the air. Wallace Stevens almost never read his poems aloud; the living tradition was revived by Dylan Thomas. The knowledge that a poetry reading is usually boring if the poet reads his written language from the written text —all of us have found that out—is one that has to be absorbed. The leaders in oral poetry have been Etheridge Knight, Bob Dylan and Allen Ginsberg, and the example of the Russians has been important. The elements were present in earlier poets, Vachel Lindsay, for example, but they seemed eccentric there. Oral poetry has now moved to the center, though it is by no means fully developed. I feel that much knowledge is lying in the Provençal, Anglo-Saxon, Greek and "primitive poets," yet to be absorbed.

One other development worth mentioning here—I'll return to it in Part Five—has nothing to do with the Orient, nor with the oral tradition, but involves a new attempt to unfold the left side of the body—I mean the emergence of the prose poem. The prose poem is the final stage of the unpretentious style, and is a raft on the Goethe stream. The prose poem is useful for renewing the narrative, and for expressing complicated human perceptions, as in the poems of Russel Edson, who is a master of it. The prose poem as developed by Francis Ponge has quite different aims. The absence of line and "ethical form" help the poet's mind to relax and so sink into the mud of earth, the water around creatures, the moist landscape of Hades, understood as the underworld. This kind of prose poem provides a psychic arena, charged but neutral, where the non-human object can live, as well as the perception of it. Such a poem has links to the work of Cézanne.

My main point is that the Novalis–Hölderlin–Goethe tradition, associated with Middle Ages alchemy, respect for the integrity of the natural world, respect for the night-intelligence, and careful observation of detail, is alive in recent poetry, much more alive than the average reader is aware.

This section holds some poems I am aware of that unfold toward mountain space, but I don't mean that this anthology includes all the good work that has been done since 1945, far from it. Because I am following one stream, I have left out examples of all the other streams, and have had to leave out many poets whom I admire tremendously. An astonishing example is Etheridge Knight, whose "Idea of Ancestry" and "The Violent Space" are as good as any poems in this book, written in English or translated. Many poets write intensely about what goes on inside a room, and so the "violet energy" of the mountain or the badger is not present. Another anthology would have to be created to include these other streams.

My head and shoulders, and my book
In the cool shade, and my body
Stretched bathing in the sun, I lie
Reading beside the waterfall—
Boehme's "Signature of all Things."
Through the deep July day the leaves
Of the laurel, all the colors
Of gold, spin down through the moving
Deep laurel shade all day. They float
On the mirrored sky and forest
For a while, and then, still slowly
Spinning, sink through the crystal deep
Of the pool to its leaf gold floor.
The saint saw the world as streaming
In the electrolysis of love.
I put him by and gaze through shade
Folded into shade of slender
Laurel trunks and leaves filled with sun.
The wren broods in her moss domed nest.
A newt struggles with a white moth
Drowning in the pool. The hawks scream,
Playing together on the ceiling
Of heaven. The long hours go by.
I think of those who have loved me,
Of all the mountains I have climbed,
Of all the seas I have swum in.
The evil of the world sinks.
My own sin and trouble fall away
Like Christian's bundle, and I watch
My forty summers fall like falling
Leaves and falling water held
Eternally in summer air.

▒   ▒   ▒

Deer are stamping in the glades,
Under the full July moon.
There is a smell of dry grass
In the air, and more faintly,
The scent of a far off skunk.
As I stand at the wood's edge,
Watching the darkness, listening
To the stillness, a small owl
Comes to the branch above me,
On wings more still than my breath.
When I turn my light on him,
His eyes glow like drops of iron,
And he perks his head at me,
Like a curious kitten.
The meadow is bright as snow.
My dog prowls the grass, a dark
Blur in the blur of brightness.
I walk to the oak grove where
The Indian village was once.
There, in blotched and cobwebbed light
And dark, dim in the blue haze,
Are twenty Holstein heifers,
Black and white, all lying down,
Quietly together, under
The huge trees rooted in the graves.

❈ ❈ ❈

When I dragged the rotten log
From the bottom of the pool,
It seemed heavy as stone.
I let it lie in the sun
For a month, and then chopped it
Into sections, and split them
For kindling, and spread them out
To dry some more. Late that night,

After reading for hours,
While moths rattled at the lamp—
The saints and the philosophers
On the destiny of man—
I went out on my cabin porch,
And looked up through the black forest
At the swaying islands of stars.
Suddenly I saw at my feet,
Spread on the floor of night, ingots
Of quivering phosphorescence,
And all about were scattered chips
Of pale cold light that was alive.

KENNETH REXROTH

Lying under the stars,
In the summer night,
Late, while the autumn
Constellations climb the sky,
As the Cluster of Hercules
Falls down the west
I put the telescope by
And watch Deneb
Move towards the zenith.
My body is asleep. Only
My eyes and brain are awake.
The stars stand around me
Like gold eyes. I can no longer
Tell where I begin and leave off.
The faint breeze in the dark pines,
And the invisible grass,
The tipping earth, the swarming stars
Have an eye that sees itself.

KENNETH REXROTH
from *The Lights in the Sky Are Stars*

Two days ago the sky was
Full of mares' tails. Yesterday
Wind came, bringing low cigar
Shaped clouds. At midnight the rain
Began, the first fine, still rain
Of autumn. Before the rain
The night was warm, the sky hazy.
We lay in the field and watched
The glowing October stars,
Vega, Deneb, Altair, high,
Hercules and the Crown setting,
The Great Nebula distinct
Through the haze. Every owl
In the world called and made love
And scolded. Once in a while
We would see one on the sky,
Cruising, on wings more silent
Than silence itself, low over
The meadow. The air thickened.
The stars grew dim and went out.
The owls stopped crying in the wood.
Then the rain came, falling so
Gently on the tent we did
Not notice until a slight
Breeze blew it in on our faces.
At dawn it was still raining.
It cleared as we cooked breakfast.
We climbed through tatters of cloud
To the east ridge and walked through
The dripping, sparkling fir forest.
In the meadow at the summit
We ate lunch in the pale sun,

Ever so slightly cooler,
And watched the same long autumn
Mares' tails and came back down the
Steep rocks through the soaking ferns.

KENNETH REXROTH
from *Mary and the Seasons*

Four Tao philosophers as cedar waxwings
chat on a February berrybush
in sun, and I am one.

Such merriment and such sobriety—
the small wild fruit on the tall stalk—
was this not always my true style?

Above an elegance of snow, beneath
a silk-blue sky a brotherhood of four
birds. Can you mistake us?

To sun, to feast, and to converse
and all together—for this I have abandoned
all my other lives.

ROBERT FRANCIS

THIS POEM IS FOR BEAR

"As for me I am a child of the god of the mountains."

A bear down under the cliff.
She is eating huckleberries.
They are ripe now
Soon it will snow, and she
Or maybe he, will crawl into a hole
And sleep. You can see
Huckleberries in bearshit if you
Look, this time of year
If I sneak up on the bear
It will grunt and run

The others had all gone down
From the blackberry brambles, but one girl
Spilled her basket, and was picking up her
Berries in the dark.
A tall man stood in the shadow, took her arm,
Led her to his home. He was a bear.
In a house under the mountain
She gave birth to slick dark children
With sharp teeth, and lived in the hollow
Mountain many years.
        snare a bear: call him out:
honey-eater
forest apple
light-foot
Old man in the fur coat, Bear! come out!
Die of your own choice!
Grandfather black-food!
        this girl married a bear

Who rules in the mountains, Bear!
        you have eaten many berries
        you have caught many fish
        you have frightened many people

Twelve species north of Mexico
Sucking their paws in the long winter
Tearing the high-strung caches down
Whining, crying, jacking off
(Odysseus was a bear)

Bear-cubs gnawing the soft tits
Teeth gritted, eyes screwed tight
        but she let them.
Till her brothers found the place
Chased her husband up the gorge

Cornered him in the rocks.
Song of the snared bear:
        "Give me my belt.
        "I am near death.
        "I come from the mountain caves
        "At the headwaters,
        "The small streams there
        "Are all dried up.

—I think I'll go hunt bears.
        "hunt bears?
Why shit Snyder,
You couldn't hit a bear in the ass
        with a handful of rice!"

GARY SNYDER

bark smells like pineapple: Jeffries
cones prick your hand: Ponderosa

nobody knows what they are, saying
"needles three to a bunch."

    turpentine tin can hangers
    high lead riggers

"the true fir cone stands straight,
the doug fir cone hangs down."

—wild pigs eat acorns in those hills
cascara cutters
tanbark oak bark gatherers
myrtlewood burl bowl-makers
little cedar dolls,
      baby girl born from the split crotch
         of a plum
           daughter of the moon—

foxtail pine with a
clipped curve-back cluster of tight
      five-needle bunches
   the rough red bark scale
and jigsaw pieces sloughed off
        scattered on the ground.
—what am I doing saying "foxtail pine"?

these conifers whose home was ice
age tundra, taiga, they of the
     naked sperm
do whitebark pine and white pine seem the same?

a sort of tree
its leaves are needles
like a fox's brush
(I call him fox because he looks that way)
and call this other thing, a
foxtail pine.

GARY SNYDER

I

Genji caught a gray bird, fluttering. It
was wounded, so I hit it with a coal shovel.
It stiffened, grew straight and symmetrical,
and began to increase in size. I took it by
the head with both hands and held it as it
swelled, turning the head from side to side.
It turned into a woman, and I was embracing
her. We walked down a dim-lighted stairway
holding hands, walking more and more swiftly
through an enormous maze, all underground.
Occasionally we touched surface, and redescended.
As we walked I kept a chart of our route in
mind—but it became increasingly complex—and
just when we reached the point where I was
about to lose my grasp of it, the woman trans-
ferred a piece of fresh-tasting apple from her
mouth to mine. Then I woke.

II

Through deep forests to the coast,
and stood on a white sandspit looking in:
over lowland swamps and prairies
where no man had ever been
to a chill view of the Olympics, in a chill clear wind.

III

We moved across dark stony ground to the great
wall: hundreds of feet high. What was beyond
it, cows?—then a thing began to rise
up from behind.

I shot my arrows, shot arrows at it, but it came—
until we turned and ran, "It's too big to
fight"—the rising thing a quarter mile across—
it was the flaming, pulsing sun. We fled and
stumbled on the bright lit plain.

IV

Where were we—
A girl in a red skirt, high heels,
going up the stairs before me in a made-over barn.
White-wash peeling, we lived together in the loft,
on cool bare boards.
—lemme tell you something kid—
     back in 1910.

V

Walking a dusty road through plowed-up fields
at forest-fire time—the fir tree hills dry,
smoke of the far fires blurred the air—
& passed on into woods, along a pond,
beneath a big red cedar,
to a bank of blinding blue wild flowers
and thick green grass on levelled ground
of hillside where your old house used to stand.
I saw the footings damp and tangled,
and thought my father was in jail,
and wondered why my mother never died,
and thought I ought to bring my sister back.

VI

High up in a yellow-gold
dry range of mountains—

brushy, rocky, cactussy hills
slowly hiking down—finally can see below,
a sea of clouds.

Lower down, always moving slowly over the
dry ground descending, can see through breaks
in the clouds: flat land.
Damp green level ricefields, farm houses,
at last to feel the heat and damp.

Descending to this humid, clouded, level world:
now I have come to the LOWLANDS.

VII

Underground building chambers clogged with refuse heaps
discarded furniture, slag, old nails,
rotting plaster, faint wisps—antique newspapers
rattle in the winds that come forever down the hall.
ladders
passing, climbing, and stopping, on from door to door.
one tiny light bulb left still burning
                —now the last—
locked *inside* is hell.
Movies going, men milling round the posters
                in shreds
                the movie always running
—we all head in here somewhere;

—years just looking for the bathrooms.
Huge and filthy, with strange-shaped toilets full of shit.
Dried shit all around, smeared across the walls of the
adjoining room,
and a vast hat track.

VIII

With Lew rode in a bus over the mountains—
rutted roads along the coast of Washington
through groves of redwood. Sitting in the
back of an almost-empty bus,
talking and riding through.
Yellow leaves fluttering down. Passing
through tiny towns at times. Damp cabins
set in dark groves of trees.
Beaches with estuaries and sandbars. I brought
a woman here once long ago,
but passed on through too quick.

IX

We were following a long river into the mountains.
Finally we rounded a bridge and could see deeper in—
the farther peaks stony and barren, a few alpine trees.
Ko-san and I stood on a point by a cliff, over a
rock-walled canyon. Ko said, "Now we have come to
where we die." I asked him, what's that up there,
then—meaning the further mountains.
"That's the world after death." I thought it looked
just like the land we'd been travelling, and couldn't
see why we should have to die.
Ko grabbed me and pulled me over the cliff—
both of us falling. I hit and I was dead. I saw
my body for a while, then it was gone. Ko was
there too. We were at the bottom of the gorge.
We started drifting up the canyon, "This is the
way to the back country."

GARY SNYDER

Rose Red's hair is brown as fur
and shines in firelight as she prepares
supper of honey and apples, curds and whey,
for the bear, and leaves it ready
on the hearth-stone.

Rose White's grey eyes
look into the dark forest.

Rose Red's cheeks are burning,
sign of her ardent, joyful
compassionate heart.
Rose White is pale,
turning away when she hears
the bear's paw on the latch.

When he enters, there is
frost on his fur,
he draws near to the fire
giving off sparks.

Rose White catches the scent of the forest,
of mushrooms, of rosin.

Together Rose Red and Rose White
sing to the bear;
it is a cradle song, a loom song,
a song about marriage, about
a pilgrimage to the mountains
long ago.
          Raised on an elbow,
the bear stretched on the hearth
nods and hums; soon he sighs
and puts down his head.

He sleeps; the Roses
bank the fire.
Sunk in the clouds of their feather bed
they prepare to dream.

Rose Red in a cave that smells of honey
dreams she is combing the fur of her cubs
with a golden comb.
Rose White is lying awake.

Rose White shall marry the bear's brother.
Shall he too
when the time is ripe,
step from the bear's hide?
Is that other, her bridegroom,
here in the room?

DENISE LEVERTOV

Come into animal presence
No man is so guileless as
the serpent. The lonely white
rabbit on the roof is a star
twitching its ears at the rain.
The llama intricately
folding its hind legs to be seated
not disdains but mildly
disregards human approval.
What joy when the insouciant
armadillo glances at us and doesn't
quicken his trotting
across the track into the palm brush.

What is this joy? That no animal
falters, but knows what it must do?
That the snake has no blemish,
that the rabbit inspects his strange surroundings
in white star-silence? The llama
rests in dignity, the armadillo
has some intention to pursue in the palm-forest.
Those who were sacred have remained so,
holiness does not dissolve, it is a presence
of bronze, only the sight that saw it
faltered and turned from it.
An old joy returns in holy presence.

DENISE LEVERTOV

THE DEPTHS

When the white fog burns off,
the abyss of everlasting light
is revealed. The last cobwebs
of fog in the
black firtrees are flakes
of white ash in the world's hearth.

Cold of the sea is counterpart
to this great fire. Plunging
out of the burning cold of ocean
we enter an ocean of intense
noon. Sacred salt
sparkles on our bodies.

After mist has wrapped us again
in fine wool, may the taste of salt
recall to us the great depths about us.

DENISE LEVERTOV

Nearly dark; warm stones of the wall in the woods
   under my hand, and now, good luck:
   a wing, with a body, glum, round, and soft,
   against the light sky; then I heard his cry:

One short cry, like a man grinding a knife in a rage,
   full of dark, melancholy, irrational contempt,
   one long, which woke reverberations in a well,
   turned down there into roots, springs, fire, rubies.

An owl sat once with his sharp hearing, his watchfulness, his
     bill,
   half-grown, majestic on my finger;
   then I felt his huge and yellow stare

plant something foreign in me, a deep quiet,
   a mad freedom; my heart laughed
   when the bird raised his soft wings.

THORKILD BJORNVIG
translated by Robert Bly

I remember gestures of infants
and they were gestures of giving me water.

    In the valley of Río Blanco
where the Aconcagua has its beginning,
I came to drink, I rushed to drink
in the fountain of a cascade,
which fell long and hard
and broke up rigid and white.
I held my mouth to the boiling spring
and the blessed water burned me,
and my mouth bled three days
from that sip from the valley of Aconcagua.

    In the fields of Mitla, a day
of harvest flies, of sun, of motion,
I bent down to a well and a native came
to hold me over the water,
and my head, like a fruit,
was within his palms.
I drank what he drank,
for his face was with my face,
and in a lightning flash I realized
I, too, was of the race of Mitla.

    On the Island of Puerto Rico,
during the slumber of full blue,
my body calm, the waves wild,
and the palms like a hundred mothers,
a child broke through skill
close to my mouth a coconut for water,
and I drank, like a daughter,
water from a mother, water from a palm.

And I have not partaken greater sweetness
with my body nor with my soul.

   At the house of my childhood
my mother brought me water.
From one sip to another sip
I saw her over the jug.
The more her head rose up
the more the jug was lowered.
I still have my valley,
I have my thirst and her vision.
This will be eternity
for we still are as we were.

I remember gestures of infants
and they were gestures of giving me water.

GABRIELA MISTRAL
translated by Gunda Kaiser

Women in black picked up their violins
　　To play, backs turned to the mirror.

The wind died as it does on the best days
　　To hear better their dark music.

But almost at once, seized by a vast amnesia,
　　The violins slumped in the women's arms

　　Like naked children fallen asleep
　　　　Among the trees.

　　Nothing it seemed could ever again stir
The motionless bows, the violins of marble,

　　And it was then that in the depths of sleep
Someone breathed to me: "You alone can do it,
　　　　Come immediately."

JULES SUPERVIELLE
translated by Geoffrey Gardner

at dusk
from the island in the river,
and it's not too cold,

I'll wait for the moon
to rise,
then take wing and glide
to meet him.

We will not speak,
but hooded against the frost
soar above
the alder flats, searching
with tawny eyes.

And then we'll sit
in the shadowy spruce and
pick the bones
of careless mice,

while the long moon drifts
toward Asia
and the river mutters
in its icy bed.

And when morning climbs
the limbs
we'll part without a sound,

fulfilled, floating
homeward as
the cold world awakens.

JOHN HAINES

Beside a narrow trail in the blue
cold of evening the trap is sprung,
and a growling deep in the throat
tells of life risen
to the surface of darkness.

The moon in my dream takes the shape
of animals who walk by its light
and never sleep, whose yellow eyes
are certain of what they seek.

Sinking, floating beneath the eyelid,
the hairy shape of the slayer appears,
a shadow that crouches
hidden in a thicket of alders,
nostrils quivering;
and the ever-deepening track
of the unseen, feeding host.

JOHN HAINES

FIRST WINTER STORM

All day long the clouds formed in the peaks,
Screening the crags,
While the pines stared through the mist.
Late-afternoon the sky hung close and black,
And when the darkness settled down,
The first large drops rapped at the roof.
In the night the wind came up and drove the rain,
Pounded at the walls with doubled fists,
And clamored in the chimney
Till I felt the fear run down my back
And grip me as I lay.

But in the morning when I looked
The sky was clear,
And all along the creeks
The cottonwoods stood somnolent and still
Beneath the sun.

WILLIAM EVERSON

Before my feet the ploughshare rolls the earth,
Up and over,
Splitting the loam with a soft tearing sound.
Between the horses I can see the red blur of a far peach orchard,
Half obscured in drifting sheets of morning fog.
A score of blackbirds circles around me on shining wings.
They alight beside me, and scramble almost under my feet
In search of upturned grubs.
The fragrance of the earth rises like tule-pond mist,
Shrouding me in impalpable folds of sweet, cool smell,
Lulling my senses to the rhythm of the running plough,
The jingle of the harness,
And the thin cries of the gleaming, bent-winged birds.

WILLIAM EVERSON

as if it were a scene made-up by the mind,
that is not mine, but is a made place,

that is mine, it is so near to the heart,
an eternal pasture folded in all thought
so that there is a hall therein

that is a made place, created by light
wherefrom the shadows that are forms fall.

Wherefrom fall all architectures I am
I say are likenesses of the First Beloved
whose flowers are flames lit to the Lady.

She it is Queen Under The Hill
whose hosts are a disturbance of words within words
that is a field folded.

It is only a dream of the grass blowing
east against the source of the sun
in an hour before the sun's going down

whose secret we see in a children's game
of ring a round of roses told.

Often I am permitted to return to a meadow
as if it were a given property of the mind
that certain bounds hold against chaos,

that is a place of first permission,
everlasting omen of what is.

ROBERT DUNCAN

THE EXPERIMENT THAT FAILED

It is probable that mutual transfusions were first performed in 1492 between
Pope Innocent VIII and two healthy boys, an experiment culminating in the
deaths of all concerned including the Pope.

Source Book of Animal Biology

I have not written my poem
about the Pope and the two young men
the obscure, muddle-headed muse
first sent when I first read
histories of the transfusion experiment.
And I do not know why,
except for the bitter fight
in me—about the fact
the boys died. (But so did he.)
The two youths look alike
in my thought. Though one is good,
one bad. Both are dead.
I may distinguish yet
between the dark and light.
One shouldn't have to kill them both.
What do we kill them with?
A knife and tourniquet?
A porcelain dish,
its wh   e flecked with dirt
            od to clot
                 nore
             r)? A tube
             ury rubber?

          e of discovery!
          ar the Catholic Columbus
        for a splendid shore
in his three, piddling ships.

161

Together they made one—
Columbus was a man.
His Canary Island docking
was an imaginative mistaking.
But what can *I* find out?
I don't even know what killed them.
Or him. And I do not want
to think it was the loss of the blood
of manhood. There is always more of that.
Besides it is really feminine
to bleed and be afraid.
Well, what then?
The one old and the two young
men. Two fresh stones, or wells—
and the powerful, untried pen.
What cut them down?
Columbus . . . Washington . . . the mythical tree . . .
the recurring blade. . . . No.
I don't see.
Yet my mind keeps holding back
with its bloody axe of stone
another idea
nobody wants known:
that it was the hope of a fresh, transmuted life
for which the Pope
and Columbus and the two sons died.

JOHN LOGAN

162

MILKWEED

While I stood here, in the open, lost in myself,
I must have looked a long time
Down the corn rows, beyond grass,
The small house,
White walls, animals lumbering toward the barn.
I look down now. It is all changed.
Whatever it was I lost, whatever I wept for
Was a wild, gentle thing, the small dark eyes
Loving me in secret.
It is here. At the touch of my hand,
The air fills with delicate creatures
From the other world.

JAMES WRIGHT

Before this longing,
I lived serene as a fish,
At one with the plants in the pond,
The mare's tail, the floating frogbit,
Among my eight-legged friends,
Open like a pool, a lesser parsnip,
Like a leech, looping myself along,
A bug-eyed edible one,
A mouth like a stickleback,—
A thing quiescent!

But now—
The wild stream, the sea itself cannot contain me:
I dive with the black hag, the cormorant,
Or walk the pebbly shore with the humpbacked heron,
Shaking out my catch in the morning sunlight,
Or rise with the gar-eagle, the great-winged condor,
Floating over the mountains,
Pitting my breast against the rushing air,
A phoenix, sure of my body,
Perpetually rising out of myself,
My wings hovering over the shorebirds,
Or beating against the black clouds of the storm,
Protecting the sea-cliffs.

THEODORE ROETHKE

—OLD MEN SLEEPING
IN SPEEDING CARS,
a hawk on a boulder
dripping with fog,
ten deer
in an autumn meadow,
yellow
aspens,
bishop pines
by the ocean.
These all speak more
as our stiff-
ness re-
laxes
into new birth.
The worth
of *things*
cracks open
and shows
the intestines.

Glittering
gold
trembling
on darkness.

MICHAEL MC CLURE

Beasts in their major freedom
Slumber in peace tonight. The gull on his ledge
Dreams in the guts of himself the moon-plucked waves below,
And the sunfish leans on a stone, slept
By the lyric water,

In which the spotless feet
Of deer make dulcet splashes, and to which
The ripped mouse, safe in the owl's talon, cries
Concordance. Here there is no such harm
And no such darkness

As the selfsame moon observes
Where, warped in window-glass, it sponsors now
The werewolf's painful change. Turning his head away
On the sweaty bolster, he tries to remember
The mood of manhood,

But lies at last, as always,
Letting it happen, the fierce fur soft to his face,
Hearing with sharper ears the wind's exciting minors,
The leaves' panic, and the degradation
Of the heavy streams.

Meantime, at high windows
Far from thicket and pad-fall, suitors of excellence
Sigh and turn from their work to construe again the painful
Beauty of heaven, the lucid moon
And the risen hunter,

Making such dreams for men
As told will break their hearts as always, bringing

Monsters into the city, crows on the public statues,
     Navies fed to the fish in the dark
          Unbridled waters.

RICHARD WILBUR

"A LAND NOT MINE"

A land not mine, still
forever memorable,
the waters of its ocean
chill and fresh.

Sand on the bottom whiter than chalk,
and the air drunk, like wine,
late sun lays bare
the rosy limbs of the pinetrees.

Sunset in the ethereal waves:
I cannot tell if the day
is ending, or the world, or if
the secret of secrets is inside me again.

ANNA AKHMATOVA
translated by Jane Kenyon

And so for nights
we waited, hoping to see
the heavy bud
    break into flower.

On its neck-like tube
hooking down from the edge
of the leaf-branch
    nearly to the floor,

the bud packed
tight with its miracle swayed
stiffly on breaths
    of air, moved

as though impelled
by stirrings within itself.
It repelled as much
    as it fascinated me

sometimes—snake,
eyeless bird head,
beak that would gape
    with grotesque life-squawk.

But you, my dear,
conceded less to the bizarre
than to the imminence
    of bloom. Yet we agreed

we ought
to celebrate the blossom,
paint ourselves, dance
    in honor of

archaic mysteries
when it appeared. Meanwhile
we waited, aware
    of rigorous design.

    Backster's
polygraph, I thought,
would have shown
    (as clearly as it had

    a philodendron's
fear) tribal sentience
in the cactus, focused
    energy of will.

    That belling of
tropic perfume—that
signalling
    not meant for us;

    the darkness
cloyed with summoning
fragrance. We dropped
    trivial tasks

    and marvelling
beheld at last the achieved
flower. Its moonlight
    petals were

    still unfold-
ing, the spike fringe of the outer
perianth recessing
    as we watched.

Lunar presence,
foredoomed, already dying,
it charged the room
        with plangency

        older than human
cries, ancient as prayers
invoking Osiris, Krishna,
        Tezcátlipóca.

        We spoke
in whispers when
we spoke
        at all . . .

ROBERT HAYDEN

A COAL FIRE IN WINTER

Something old and tyrannical burning there.
(Not like a wood fire which is only
The end of a summer, or a life)
But something of darkness: heat
From the time before there was fire.
And I have come here
To warm that blackness into forms of light,
To set free a captive prince
From the sunken kingdom of the father coal.

A warming company of the cold-blooded—
These carbon serpents of bituminous gardens,
These inflammable tunnels of dead song from the black pit,
This sparkling end of the great beasts, these blazing
Stone flowers diamond fire incandescent fruit.
And out of all that death, now,
At midnight, my love and I are riding
Down the old high roads of inexhaustible light.

THOMAS MCGRATH

Alone on the jagged rock at the south end of McClure's
Beach. The sky low. The sea grows more and more private, as
afternoon goes on, the sky comes down closer, the unobserved
water rushes out to the horizon, horses galloping in a mountain
valley at night. The waves smash up the rock, I find flags of
seaweed high on the worn top, forty feet up, thrown up
overnight, separated water still pooled there, like the black ducks
that fly desolate, forlorn, and joyful over the seething swells,
who never "feel pity for themselves," and "do not lie awake
weeping for their sins." In their blood cells the vultures coast with
furry necks extended, watching over the desert for signs of life
to end. It is not our life we need to weep for. Inside us there is
some secret. We are following a narrow ledge around a mountain,
we are sailing on skeletal eerie craft over the buoyant ocean.

ROBERT BLY

for Lewis Thomas, and *The Lives of the Cell*

My friend, this body is made of bone and excited protozoa . . . and it is with my body that I love the fields. How do I know what I feel but what the body tells me? Erasmus thinking in the snow, translators of Virgil who burn up the whole room, the man in furs reading the Arabic astrologer falls off his three-legged stool in astonishment, this is the body, so beautifully carved inside, with the curves of the inner ear, and the husk so rough, knuckle-brown.

As we walk, we enter the fields of other bodies, and every smell we take in the communities of protozoa see, and a being inside leaps up toward it, as a horse rears at the starting gate. When we come near each other, we are drawn down into the sweetest pools of slowly circling smells . . . slowly circling energies . . . The protozoa know there are odors the shape of oranges, of tornadoes, or octopuses . . .

> *The sunlight lays itself down before every protozoa,*
> *the night opens itself out behind it,*
> *and inside its own energy it lives!*

So the space between two people diminishes, it grows less and less, no one to weep, they merge at last. The sound that pours from the fingertips awakens clouds of cells far inside the body, and beings unknown to us start out in a pilgrimage to their Saviour, to their holy place. Their holy place is a small black stone, that they remember from Protozoic times, when it was rolled away from a door . . . and it was after that they found their friends, who helped them to digest the hard grains of this world . . . The cloud of cells awakens, intensifies, swarms . . . the beings dance inside beams of sunlight so thin we cannot see them . . . to them each ray is a vast palace, with thousands of rooms. From the dance of

the cells praise sentences rise to the voice of the man praying
and singing alone in his room. He lets his arms climb above his
head, and says, "Now do you still say you cannot choose
the road?"

ROBERT BLY

1. I wake in the night,
   An old ache in the shoulder blades.
   I lie amazed under the trees
   That creak a little in the dark,
   The giant trees of the world.

   I lie on earth the way
   Flames lie in the woodpile,
   Or as an imprint, in sperm, of what is to be.
   I love the earth, and always
   In its darknesses I am a stranger.

2. 6 A.M. Water frozen again. Melted it and made tea. Ate a
   raw egg and the last orange. Refreshed by a long sleep. The
   trail practically indistinguishable under 8″ of snow. 9:30 A.M.
   Snow up to my knees in places. Sweat begins freezing under
   my shirt when I stop to rest. The woods are filled, anyway,
   with the windy noise of the first streams. 10:30 A.M. The sun
   at last. The snow starts to melt off the boughs at once,
   falling with little ticking sounds. Mist clouds are lying in
   the valleys. 11:45 A.M. Slow, glittering breakers roll in on the
   beaches ten miles away, very blue and calm. Odd to see it
   while sitting in snow. 12 noon. An inexplicable sense of joy,
   as if some happy news had been transmitted to me directly,
   bypassing the brain. 2 P.M. From the top of Gauldy I looked
   back into Hebo valley. Castle Rock sticks into a cloud. A cool
   breeze comes up from the valley, it is a fresh, earthly wind
   and tastes of snow and trees. It is not like those transcendental
   breezes that make the heart ache. It brings happiness. 2:30 P.M.
   Lost the trail. A woodpecker watches me wade through the
   snow trying to locate it. The sun has gone back of the trees.
   3:10 P.M. Still hunting for the trail. Getting cold. From an
   elevation I have an open view of the SE, a world of timberless,

white hills, rolling, weirdly wrinkled. Above them a pale
half moon. 3:45 P.M. Going on by map and compass. I saw
a deer a minute ago, he fled touching down every fifteen feet
or so. 7:30 P.M. Made camp near the head of Alder Creek.
Trampled a bed into the snow and filled it with boughs.
Concocted a little fire in the darkness. Ate pork and beans.
A slug or two of whisky burnt my throat. The night very
clear. Very cold. That half moon is up there and a lot of stars
have come out among the treetops. The fire has fallen to coals.

3. The coals go out,
    The last smoke weaves up
    Losing itself in the stars.
    This is my first night to lie
    In the uncreating dark.

    In the heart of a man
    There sleeps a green worm
    That has spun the heart about itself,
    And that shall dream itself black wings
    One day to break free into the beautiful black sky.

    I leave my eyes open,
    I lie here and forget our life,
    All I see is we float out
    Into the emptiness, among the great stars,
    On this little vessel without lights.

    I know that I love the day,
    The sun on the mountain, the Pacific
    Shiny and accomplishing itself in breakers,
    But I know I live half alive in the world,
    I know half my life belongs to the wild darkness.

GALWAY KINNELL

When despair for the world grows in me
and I wake in the night at the least sound
in fear of what my life and my children's lives may be,
I go and lie down where the wood drake
rests in his beauty on the water, and the great heron feeds.
I come into the peace of wild things
who do not tax their lives with forethought
of grief. I come into the presence of still water.
And I feel above me the day-blind stars
waiting with their light. For a time
I rest in the grace of the world, and am free.

WENDELL BERRY

Mother of my birth, for how long were we together
in your love and my adoration of your self?
For the shadow of a moment as I breathed your pain
and you breathed my suffering, as we knew
of shadows in lit rooms that would swallow the light.

Your face beneath the oxygen tent was alive
but your eyes were closed. Your breathing was hoarse
but your sleep was with death. I was alone with you
as it was when I was young but only alone now
and not with you. I was to be alone forever
as I was learning, watching you become alone.

Earth is your mother as you were mine, my earth,
my sustenance, my comfort and my strength
and now without you I turn to your mother
and seek from her that I may meet you again
in rock and stone: whisper to the stone,
I love you; whisper to the rock, I found you;
whisper to earth, Mother, I have found my mother
and I am safe and always have been.

DAVID IGNATOW

Darkmotherscream is a Siberian dance,
cry from prison or a yell for help,
or, perhaps, God has another word for it—
ominous little grin—darkmotherscream.

Darkmotherscream is the ecstasy of the sexual gut;
We let the past sink into darkmotherscream also.
You, we—oooh with her eyes closed
woman moans in ecstasy—darkmother, darkmotherscream.

Darkmotherscream is the original mother of languages.
It is silly to trust mind, silly to argue against it.
Prognosticating by computers
We leave out darkmotherscream.

"How's it going?" Darkmotherscream.
"Motherscream! Motherscream!"
            "OK, we'll do it, we'll do it."

The teachers can't handle darkmotherscream.
That is why Lermontov is untranslatable.
When the storm sang in Yelabuga,
What did it say to her? Darkmotherscream.

Meanwhile go on dancing, drunker and drunker.
"Shagadam magadam—darkmotherscream."
Don't forget—Rome fell
not having grasped the phrase: darkmotherscream.

ANDREI VOZNESENSKY
translated by Robert Bly and Vera Dunham

It is people at the edge who say
things at the edge: winter is toward knowing.

    Sled runners before they meet have long talk apart.
    There is a pup in every litter the wolves will have.
    A knife that falls points at an enemy.
    Rocks in the wind know their place: down low.
    Over your shoulder is God; the dying deer sees Him.

At the mouth of the long sack we fall in forever
storms brighten the spikes of the stars.

    Wind that buried bear skulls north of here
    and beats moth wings for help outside the door
    is bringing bear skull wisdom, but do not ask the skull
    too large a question till summer.
    Something too dark was held in that strong bone.

Better to end with a lucky saying:

    Sled runners cannot decide to join or to part.
    When they decide, it is a bad day.

WILLIAM STAFFORD

In the Aztec design God crowds
into the little pea that is rolling
out of the picture.
All the rest extends bleaker
because God has gone away.

In the White Man design, though,
no pea is there.
God is everywhere,
but hard to see.
The Aztecs frown at this.

How do you know he is everywhere?
And how did he get out of the pea?

WILLIAM STAFFORD

The ranchers are selling their wheat early this year, not holding
it over for a better price in the Spring. Next year the government
lifts restrictions on planting, and nobody is sure what will
happen when wheat grows "fencerow to fencerow." This
morning another man has come out from the Grain Growers to
help us out. John and I haven't got time to cooper boxcars and
handle trucks too.

At lunchtime, he takes his carpenter's apron off and sits on a
grain door in the shade of a boxcar, resting before he eats. I go out
to join him and notice a Bible resting on the ledge under the
rear window of his car. He says he doesn't read it much, and
because he is anxious not to appear narrowly Christian, I want to
know more about him. He is sixty-five, about to retire; a lonely
man, it seems. There is something unspoken in him. His eyes
squint to keep out the bright sunlight falling now just where the
boxcar's shadow stops. I say, "There's one thing in Mark that has
always puzzled me." He turns to face me, and I continue. "Where
Jesus says, *To them that have shall be given, and from them that
have not shall be taken away.* That always seemed cruel to me,
but since the verb hasn't got an object (have what? have not
what?) if you supply an object, it's really alive. Love. Money.
Intelligence. Curiosity. Anything."

In the bleached countryside of his mind, suddenly a new
season washes over; common plants begin to blossom. And now,
ideas fly back and forth between us, like bees, their legs thickening
with pollen.

In the next hour we talk a lot and I learn that he has been
reading Rufus Jones, Meister Eckhart, and *The Cloud of
Unknowing.* He nearly trembles with a new joy he kept hidden.
His wife writes poetry, he tells me, and adds—thrusting years
recklessly aside—"I've worked here sixteen years, one harvest to
another. I've seen a lot of young men come and go, and never

183

had a decent conversation. It's worse with the college kids. They don't think, most of them."

Trucks start coming in again, lunch is over. He puts his carpenter's apron on again, but before we part he invites me home to dinner this evening, careful not to spoil it by appearing as happy as he really is.

Back inside the elevator, I'd like to lie down somewhere in a cool, dark corner, and weep. What are people doing with their lives? what are they doing?

ROBERT SUND

Even now this landscape is assembling.
The hills darken. The oxen
sleep in their blue yoke,
the fields having been
picked clean, the sheaves
bound evenly and piled at the roadside
among cinquefoil, as the toothed moon rises:

This is the barrenness
of harvest or pestilence.
And the wife leaning out the window
with her hand extended, as in payment,
and the seeds
distinct, gold, calling
Come here
Come here, little one

And the soul creeps out of the tree.

LOUISE GLÜCK

as darkness
is my shelter
i shall not
want.
it leads me
deep
into the bones
of men.

as darkness
is my shelter
i find the knees
of my mother
among the stairways
of stars,
my father's forehead
among the blind
sisters who sing
behind
the sunset.

i find
my eyes
in the dim
thigh of the dew
and i fall
among shadows
forever.

weightless
as
the dying
moth

and the dusk
leads me
into the eye of the owl,
my poems,
bright rats
sliding
in the rivers
of wet grass.

i love
the snakes,
who hunt at night,
awakened
by the cooling earth
and
who emerge, slick
genital
faces
from the dark
mouth.

GREGORY HALL

Just as the small waves came where no waves were,
unending as the peaceful turn of fish,
breaking the still level of the morning
until by noon we half forgot the sea
had ever been a taut and hazy skin,

so resting on the shore we kept the motion.
At calm we found we rocked in air
the long day's waves, were not surprised
come evening we played whale, spewed softened brine,
rolled effortless and mammoth through the night.

PAMELA MILLWARD

a transformation

She stood
apart from the grazing herd
motionless,
except for a slowed
curl of her trunk,
her head lowered,
her great ears flopped forward
like a closing umbrella
as the bull
came to sniff.

When she dropped to her haunches,
the herd
screaming and trumpeting,
thundered,
a fallen half-moon
around her.

Her forelegs collapsed
and she slumped to her belly,
a Dagon come tumbling down.
Only the young ones
were allowed
to touch her now:
one laid his trunk on her back;
one nuzzled her ear;
one strained at her great fallen rump
as if pushing toward life
and learning of death.

Then the great bull,
head lowered,

tried to lift her with a roar.
He moved to her head and tried to lift her.
He tore a trunkful of dry grass
and stuffed it in her mouth
over the dust on her sagged lip
to lift her.
He tried to mount her into life.
She heaved to her side
and was dead.

It was sunset
late African spring
and December,
as a restless
feeding herd came
one by one to the gray body
and moved off
together over the ridge
into the dusk.

GIANFRANCO PAGNUCCI

V

Before they ripen into diffused spirits
angels are leaf-stalks
and their wings begonia leaves
with dark surfaces
and red glitterings within.
Slowly, very slowly, they emerge out of the flower-pot
of the body,
take on the face of Bill or Bob,
pierce through the cool bower
of the world
and ascend like the promise
of a harmonious end;
on their lips shine
the last bubbles of our breathing,
those droplets
of our unrelieved loneliness.

KATERINA ANGHELAKI-ROOKE
from *The Angelic Poems*
translated by Kimon Friar

Saw a lamb being born.
Saw the shepherd chase and grab a big ewe
and dump her on her side.
Saw him rub some stuff from a bottle on his hands.
Saw him bend and reach in.
Heard two cries from the ewe.
Two sharp quick cries. Like high grunts.
Saw him pull out a slack white package.
Saw him lay it out on the ground.
Saw him kneel and take his teeth to the cord.
Saw him slap the package around.
Saw it not move.
Saw him bend and put his mouth to it and blow.
Doing this calmly, half kneeling.
Saw him slap it around some more.
Saw my mother watching this. Saw Angela. Saw Peter.
Saw Mimi, with a baby in her belly.
Saw them standing in a row
by the dry stone wall, in the wind.
Saw the package move.
Saw it was stained with red and yellow.
Saw the shepherd wipe red hands on the ewe's wool.
Heard the other sheep in the meadow calling out.
Saw the package shaking its head.
Saw it try to stand. Saw it nearly succeed.
Saw it have to sit and think about it a bit.
Saw a new creature's first moments of thinking.
Felt the chill blowing through me.
Heard the shepherd say:
"Good day for lambing. Wind dries them out."
Saw the package start to stand. Get half-way. Kneeling.

Saw it push upward. Stagger, push. And make it.
Stand, standing.
Saw it surely was a lamb, a lamb, a lamb.
Saw a lamb being born!

MICHAEL DENNIS BROWNE

White hard rock
altered from that serpentine body
by hot waters, no one knows just how,
metamorphosed from your earlier life
who would guess you're descended from that
green lustrous material
the Indians carved for pipes or rubbed in their hands
to gladden the spirits. You're silicified so completely
you look like knobby white chert
badly fractured from your earlier hydrated beginning.
Your story isn't often told
how you had an even earlier origin in the earth's mantle
you rode up a subduction zone
for your first intrusion and now you're in my backyard.
At first I thought you were an outcrop
before I climbed in the cellars of Easter Walk
and found the hill was made of Franciscan graywacke,
badly fractured. Later I discovered
you had no connections
deep down you were a big rolling stone
from Cragmont Rock.

I've been sitting on you several hours
silica carbonate rock you remain
as imprecise as your name
I'd start if anybody called me
flesh bones man.
I wonder what others sat here before me
on you in this garden, sunset,
birds I never met before
act like this is their home.

FRED BERRY

194

Don't be afraid of dying. The glass of water
Is quickly poured into the waiting goblet.

Your face that will be of no further use to mirrors
Grows more and more transparent, nothing is hidden.

It's night in the remotest provinces of the brain,
Seeing falls back into the great sea of light.

How strange to see that glittering green fly
Walk onto the eyeball, rubbing its hands and praying.

Don't be afraid, you're going to where you were
Before birth pushed you into this cold light.

Lie down here, next to Empedocles;
Be joined to the small grains of the brotherhood.

ROBERT MEZEY

I thought the earth
remembered me, she
took me back so tenderly, arranging
her dark skirts, her pockets
full of lichens and seeds. I slept
as never before, a stone
on the riverbed, nothing
between me and the white fire of the stars
but my thoughts, and they floated
light as moths among the branches
of the perfect trees. All night
I heard the small kingdoms breathing
around me, the insects, and the birds
who do their work in the darkness. All night
I rose and fell, as if in water, grappling
with a luminous doom. By morning
I had vanished at least a dozen times
into something better.

MARY OLIVER

In the riprap,
   in the cool caves,
      in the dim and salt-refreshed
         recesses, they cling
in dark clusters,
   in barnacled fistfuls,
      in the dampness that never
         leaves, in the deeps
of high tide, in the slow
   washing away of the water
      in which they feed,
         in which the blue shells
open a little, and the orange bodies
   make a sound,
      not loud,
         not unmusical, as they take
nourishment, as the ocean
   enters their bodies. At low tide
      I am on the riprap, clattering
         with boots and a pail,
rock over rock; I choose
   the crevice, I reach
      forward into the dampness,
         my hands feeling everywhere
for the best, the biggest. Even before
   I decide which to take,
      which to twist from the wet rocks,
         which to devour,
they, who have no eyes to see with,
   see me, like a shadow,
      bending forward. Together
         they make a sound,

not loud,
    not unmusical, as they lean
      into the rocks, away
        from my grasping fingers.

MARY OLIVER

198

If you want to live in the country you have to understand the
    power of maples.
You have to see them sink their teeth into the roots of the old
    locusts.
You have to see them force the sycamores to gasp for air.
You have to see them move their thick hairs into the cellar.
    And when you cut your great green shad pole
you have to be ready for it to start sprouting in your hands;
you have to stick it in the ground like a piece of willow;
you have to plant your table under its leaves and begin eating.

GERALD STERN

DIFFERENCES

coughing up blood
before the sun rose.

i spit out the wind
and all turns into
what might be expected
on a rainy day. sleep.

i dreamed of an animal
with its teeth shining
so greatly . . .

and we have heard from
each other once or twice.
we seek to see who is god.

RAY YOUNG BEAR

The headstones are thin; the trees are thick—
   old, rough-skinned maples.
This small cemetery is a cool green place for the dead
   to journey out of themselves out of sight,
   to leave the script of their bones in the earth.
Beyond the low iron fence, cows graze,
   crunch grass and gaze,
   flicking away flies with the frayed ropes of their tails.
Swaying bags of milk hang from their bodies.
Their groaning voices, buried in the muscles of the throat,
   are not used often.
The black and white hides shine over the deep meat,
   the blood and bones.
The cows drift nearer. . . .
All that brute flesh wandering close to graves—
   how calm it is—
   like two hands about to touch.

HOWARD NELSON

I

Outside New York, a high place where with one glance you take
in the houses where eight million human beings live.
The giant city over there is a long flimmery drift, a spiral galaxy
seen from the side.
Inside the galaxy, coffee cups are being pushed across the desk,
department store windows hold out a begging cup, a whirlwind
of shoes that leave no trace behind.
Firescapes climbing up, elevator doors that silently close, behind
triple-locked doors a steady swell of voices.
Slumped over bodies doze in the subway cars, catacombs in
motion.
I know also—statistics to the side—that at this instant down
there Schubert is being played in some room, and for that
person the notes are more real than all the rest.

II

The immense treeless plains of the human brain have gotten
folded and refolded 'til they are the size of a fist.
The swallow in April returns to its last year's nest under the
eaves in precisely the right barn in precisely the right
township.
She flies from the Transvaal, passes the equator, flies for six
weeks over two continents, navigates toward precisely this
one disappearing dot in the landmass.
And the man who gathers up the signals from a whole lifetime
into a few perfectly ordinary chords for five string musicians,
the one who got a river to flow through the eye of a needle
is a plump young man from Vienna, his friends called him "The
Mushroom," who slept with his glasses on
and every morning punctually stood at his high writing table.

When he did that the strange hundred-footed notes started to
move on the page.

III

The five bowers are bowing. I go home through warm woods
where the earth is springy under my feet
curl up like someone still unborn, sleep, roll on so weightlessly
into the future, suddenly understand that plants are thinking.

IV

How much we have to take on trust every minute we live in
order not to drop through the earth!
Take on trust the snow masses clinging to rocksides over the town.
Take on trust the unspoken promises, and the smile of agreement,
trust that the telegram does not concern us,
and that the sudden ax blow from inside is not coming.
Trust the axles we ride on down the thruway among the swarm
of steel bees magnified three hundred times.
But none of that stuff is really worth the trust we have.
The five string instruments say that we can take something
else on trust, and they walk with us a bit on that road.
As when the light bulb goes out on the stair, and the hand
follows—trusting it—the blind banister rail that finds its
way in the dark.

V

We crowd up onto the piano stool and play four-handed in
F-Minor, two drivers for the same carriage, it looks a little
ridiculous.
It looks as if the hands are moving weights made of sound back
and forth, as if we were moving lead weights
in an attempt to alter the big scale's frightening balance, so that:
happiness and suffering should weigh exactly the same.
Annie said: "This music is so heroic," and she is right.

But those who glance enviously at men of action, people who
    despise themselves inside for not being murderers,
do not find themselves in this music.
And the people who buy and sell others, and who believe that
    everyone can be bought, don't find themselves here.
Not their music. The long melody line that remains itself
    among all its variations, sometimes shiny and gentle, some-
    times rough and powerful, the snail's trace and steel wire.
The stubborn humming sound that this instant is with us
upward into
The depths.

TOMAS TRANSTRÖMER
translated by Robert Bly

Images drip down my back like sweat.
From this hunger I can see time.
Dreams float in deep green whirls under that fog.
Four brown bears stepped through,
mist washing around them like steam
or old reluctant spirits.
We bowed in a ritual I did not know I knew.
A white woman stumbled slowly past
children bent her long pale back.
Her blue eyes opened like the sun
and two white scars sunk through my chest.
The bears shuffled close, shook their manes
and waved their heavy arms against her.
She dropped the children and they grew like gods.
Bear smell thickened, they backed around me like walls.
She touched the bears and they were stone.
She stacked them down there by the creek,
her children standing guard like pillars.
and her breasts hanging golden in the sun.
She lumbers up the hill, low to the ground,
her hot skin wet under mud and matted fur of bear.
Tonight she comes for me.

W. M. RANSOM

I sit down at a table and open a book of poems and move slowly into the shadows of tall trees. They are white pines I think. The ground is covered with soft brown needles and there are signs that animals have come here silently and vanished before I could catch sight of them. But here the trail edges into a cedar swamp; wet ground, deadfall and rotting leaves. I move carefully but rapidly, pleased with myself.

Someone else comes and sits down at the table, a serious looking young man with a large stack of books. He takes a book from the top of the stack and opens it. The book is called *How to Get a High Paying Job*. He flips through it and lays it down and picks up another and pages through it quickly. It is titled *Moving Ahead*.

We are moving ahead very rapidly now, through a second growth of popple and birch, our faces scratched and our clothes torn by the underbrush. We are moving even faster now, marking the trail, followed closely by bulldozers and crews with chain saws and representatives of the paper company.

LOUIS JENKINS

It is best to turn on the set only after all the stations have gone
off the air and just watch the snow fall. This is the other life you
have been promising yourself. Somewhere back in the woods,
ten miles from the nearest town and that just a wide place in the
road with a tavern and gas station. When you drive home,
after midnight, half drunk, the roads are treacherous. And your
wife is home alone, worried, looking anxiously out at the snow.
This snow has been falling steadily for days, so steadily the
snow plows can't keep up. So you drive slow, peering down the
road. And there! Did you see it? Just at the edge of your headlight
beams, something, a large animal, or a man, crossed the road.
Stop. There he is among the birches, a tall man wearing a white
suit. No, it isn't a man. Whatever it is—it motions to you,
an almost human gesture, then retreats farther into the woods.
He stops and motions again. The snow is piling up all around the
car. Are you coming?

LOUIS JENKINS

Part five:
The object poem

The trouble with most poetry is that
it is either subjective or objective.

Basho

IN THE LAST sixty years, a wonderful new poem has appeared. It is the object poem, or thing poem. One can find scattered examples throughout European literature, but the poem has gathered force only in the last few decades, associated primarily with the "seeing" poems of Rilke, and the "object" poems of Francis Ponge.

Rilke was Rodin's secretary for a while, and Rodin one day advised him to go down to the zoo and try to *see* something. Rilke did, and spent some time watching a panther. Rodin respected *seeing*, the ability to observe, to use the terrific energy of the eyes, to pay attention to something besides one's own subjectivity. Rilke understood that his own poetry lacked seeing, and he wrote nearly two hundred poems in about six years in an effort to sharpen his seeing. Through that labor, Rilke passed to a new stage of his art. Strangely, Novalis in 1800 had spoken of this passage. Novalis thought there were two stages in an artist's life:

> *Self-expression is the source of all abasement, just as, contrariwise, it is the basis for all true elevation. The first step is introspection—exclusive contemplation of the self. But whoever stops there goes only half way. The second step must be genuine observation outward—spontaneous, sober observation of the external world.*

Putting the words "sober" and "spontaneous" together is interesting. The Sixties longed for spontaneous observation, but didn't understand the sober part; the longing to be excited all the time is probably a form of narcissism. If a poet remains stuck in the first stage, the introspective, narcissistic stage, he or she is essentially a sun surrounded by dead planets, to borrow Novalis' concept "Man is a sun, and his senses are the planets." Psychologists often are suns surrounded by dead planets. We all use our senses, but if the senses are called upon only to embody intuitions about ourselves, they die. The senses long to experience objects and things on their own; they don't want to be slaves of our intuition.

Scientists often respect their senses, and some, especially biologists, use them more intensely than many contemporary poets. Perhaps, as someone said, the second stage for scientists is introspection.

The discipline Rilke learned carried him farther into his own body, and farther out into the world. He watched a panther at the zoo, and his German lines, in rhythm and sound, embody movingly the repetitive, desperate walk of the panther. By the end of the poem he is somehow inside the panther's body. Each time the panther glimpses a shape, say a dog or a child, the image goes to the body's center, the place from which a leap begins; but no leap can take place. A leap can't take place, and so the image "reaches the heart, and dies."

Few artists follow Rilke's road into the second stage. Dürer's watercolors of fir trees and a clump of grass clearly are second stage art, and some contemporary art, and some Chinese landscape. It's possible that mass culture traps people in the first stage or even in a pre-firststage, a pre-introspective state. We develop a "culture of narcissism." Advertisements on television encourage the human being to follow his body's whims, and finally one believes that the Montana hills were created to provide oil for central heating. Mass culture encourages the comfort of not-seeing. So when an artist moves into the second stage, the audience trained on mass culture often becomes upset; and Rilke lost many of his readers when he went into the seeing poems. To the end of his life, most German readers preferred his first book. Rilke, however, continued in that arc, and besides the two hundred or so seeing poems he wrote for

Neue Gedichte, a large number of his uncollected poems, written from 1906 to 1926, are seeing poems. I've included one poem here from that group, on the palm of the hand. The language has such fragrance that the poem seems an intuitive accident, but it is impossible without his years of seeing.

J. Hillis Miller in *Poets of Reality* writes about the longing, usually frustrated, for union with the object among mid-nineteenth-century poets like Tennyson. Mr. Miller describes so beautifully their sensation, which was that once they became convinced that God was absent or dead, objects disappeared. "God seems to Tennyson, to Arnold, or to the early Hopkins to have withdrawn beyond the physical world. For such poets God still exists, but he is no longer present in nature." I think the writing of the object poem implies that we have the longing to give honor to objects again, and that we don't feel them so distant. It also implies that matter is not simply to be dismissed as matter. Nothing could be more opposite to Rilke's point of view than certain unbalanced pro-spirit statements one often hears in Christian or Oriental groups. In each Christian Science service today, the following paragraph is spoken:

> *There is no life, truth, substance, nor intelligence in matter. All is infinite mind, and its infinite manifestation, for God is all in all.*
>
> *Spirit is immortal truth; matter is mortal error. Spirit is real, and eternal; matter is unreal and temporal.*
>
> *Spirit is God, and man is his image and likeness. Therefore man is not material, he is spiritual.*

This is an astounding slander of matter. No person who believes this could write a thing poem.

The second poet of matter, or master of the thing poem, is Francis Ponge, a French civil servant, still alive. Ponge adopted primarily the prose poem form for his thing poems. The prose poem is associated with the second stage, perhaps because great detail is possible when the object is being described. Something surprising happens often during the writing. It is as if the object itself, a stump or an orange, has links with the human psyche, and the unconscious provides material it would not give if asked directly. The unconscious passes into the object and returns. The union of the object with the psyche moves slowly, and the poem may take four or five years to write. Ponge's book, called *Le Parti Pris des Choses*, was written over twenty years and was published in 1942. The title means "taking the side of things." It suggests that Ponge is refusing to exploit things, either as symbols or as beings of a lower class. The title also suggests another meaning: that the things themselves have opinions, or points of view. Ponge has confidence that things are fruitful and nourishing, not hostile, not emptied of spirit, not inferior, not unreal. We sense that Cézanne's work carries a similar faith.

Ponge says that true poetry has very little in common with "what one sees in the poetry anthologies of today." Reading anthologies, we notice that the vast majority of poems written in this century pay no attention to any object, do not evoke objects or give them honor. The poet dispenses with the object and begins immediately with "I." "There is a kernel of hate in me," or "My grandmother in her old picture resembles me." If the poem does begin with an object, the poet usually—I have done this often—leaves it part way through to return to the "I." Ponge in general remains near the object all the way through the poem. That ability is astonishing. The concentration in his poem, "Trees Abandon Something Inside a Circle of Fog" remains on trees throughout, even on the bodily experiences a tree goes through in fall. It's possible that Ponge has some perception about girls and marriage in mind, but the last syllable is as true to the tree's physical experience as the first. It's astonishing. And how many people— how many poets—have opened the same door, thousands of times each year, somehow without noticing it? Or perhaps they don't believe the door worthy of honor. Francis Ponge, so far as I know, has written the only poem on opening a door, and it is brilliant in every line. Ponge doesn't try to be cool, distant, or objective, nor "let the object speak for itself." His poems are funny, his vocabulary immense, his personality full of quirks, and yet the poem remains somewhere in the place where the senses join the object. "The seat of the soul is where the inner world and the outer world meet, and where they overlap, it is in every point of the overlap," in Novalis' words.

In 1952, Ponge published an essay on poetry called "The Silent World Is Our Only Homeland." I'll quote a part of this rich essay, which can be found in entirety in Beth Archer's book, *The Voice of Things*.

> *In these terms, one will surely understand what I consider to be the function of poetry. It is to nourish the spirit of man by giving him the cosmos to suckle. We have only to lower our standard of dominating nature and to raise our standard of participating in it in order to make the reconciliation take place. When man becomes proud to be not just the site where ideas and feelings are produced, but also the crossroad where they divide and mingle, he will be ready to be saved. Hope there-fore lies in a poetry through which the world so invades the spirit of man that he becomes almost speechless, and later reinvents a language. Poets should in no way concern themselves with human relationships, but should get to the very bottom. Society, furthermore, takes good care of putting them there, and the love of things keeps them there; they are the ambassadors of the silent world. As such, they stammer, they murmur, they sink into the darkness of logos—until at last they reach the level of ROOTS, where things and formulas are one.*
>
> *This is why, whatever one says, poetry is much more important than any other art, any other science. This is also why poetry has nothing in common with what appears in the poetry anthologies of today. True poetry is what does not pretend to be poetry. It is in the dogged drafts of a few maniacs seeking the new encounter.*

I don't agree with his remark about relationships, but everything else I like. A few years later, he wrote a poem called "This Is Why I Have Lived." He has left a place inside his poems for things:

> *I stretched out*
> *alongside beings and things . . .*
>
> *I have written, it has been published, I have lived,*
> *I have written, they have lived, I have lived.*

(Beth Archer's translation)

Kings don't touch doors.

They don't know this joy: to push affectionately or fiercely before us one of those huge panels we know so well, then to turn back in order to replace it—holding a door in our arms.

The pleasure of grabbing one of those tall barriers to a room abdominally, by its porcelain knot; of this swift fighting, body-to-body, when, the forward motion for an instant halted, the eye opens and the whole body adjusts to its new surroundings.

But it still keeps one friendly hand on the door, holding it open, then decisively pushes it away, closing itself in—which the click of the powerful but well-oiled spring pleasantly confirms.

FRANCIS PONGE
translated by Robert Bly

The oyster, about as large as a medium-sized stone, has a
rougher look, and a less consistent color, whitish in a dazzling
way. It is a world bull-headedly sealed. You can open it, however;
you must hold it then in the deep fold of a napkin, use a knife
notched and not too honest, and try more than once. Fingers
that are curious cut themselves, break their nails: it's not an
elegant task. The knocks you give it leave whitish rings on the
shell, halos of some kind.

Once inside, you will find an entire world, for drinking and
for eating: beneath a *firmament* (to speak properly) of mother-
of-pearl, the upper heavens slowly approach the lower heavens,
making what is really only a pool, a viscous and greenish pillow
that rises and falls as you smell and look, decorated at the edges
with a fringe of blackish lace.

Occasionally—it is rare—a beautiful expression rises in their
mother-of-pearl throats, and you find good reason then to adorn
yourself.

FRANCIS PONGE
translated by Robert Bly

Inside the fog that encloses the trees, they undergo the robbing of their leaves . . . Thrown into confusion by a slow oxidation, and humiliated by the sap's withdrawal for the sake of the flowers and fruits, the leaves, following the hot spells of August, cling less anyway.

The up-and-down tunnels inside the bark deepen, and guide the moisture down to earth so as to break off with the animated parts of the tree.

The flowers are scattered, the fruits taken away. This giving up of their more animated parts, and even of parts of their body, has become, since their earliest days, a familiar practice for trees.

FRANCIS PONGE
translated by Robert Bly

Many times the size of man, the horse has flaring nostrils, round eyes under half-closed lids, cocked ears and long muscular neck.

The tallest of man's domestic animals, and truly his designated mount.

Man, somewhat lost on an elephant, is at his best on a horse, truly a throne to his measure.

We will not do away with the horse, I hope?

He will not become a curiosity in a zoo?

. . . Already now, in town, he is no more than a miserable substitute for the automobile, the most miserable means of traction.

Ah, the horse is also—does man suspect it?—something else besides! He is *impatience* nostrilized.

His weapons are running, biting, bucking.

He seems to have a keen nose, keen ears, and very sensitive eyes.

The greatest tribute one can pay him is having to fit him with blinders.

But no weapon . . .

Whereby the temptation to add one. One only. A horn.

Thereby the unicorn.

The horse, terribly nervous, is aerophagous.

Hypersensitive, he clamps his jaws, holds his breath, then releases it, making the walls of his nasal cavities vibrate loudly.

That is why this noble beast, who feeds on air and grass alone, produces only straw turds and thunderous fragrant farts.

Fragrant thunderisms.

What am I saying, feeds on air? Gets drunk on it. Sniffs it, savors it, snorts it.

He rushes into it, shakes his mane in it, kicks up his hind legs in it.

He would evidently like to fly up in it.
The flight of clouds inspires him, urges him to imitation.
He does imitate it: he tosses, prances . . .
And when the whip's lightning claps, the clouds gallop
faster and rain tramples the earth . . .

Out of your stall, high-spirited over-sensitive armoire, all
polished and smoothed!
Great beautiful period piece!
Polished ebony or mahogany.
Stroke the withers of this armoire and immediately it has a
faraway look.
Dust cloth at the lips, feather mop at the rump, key in the
lock of the nostrils.
His skin quivers, irritably tolerating flies, his shoe hammers
the ground.
He lowers his head, leans his muzzle toward the ground and
consoles himself with grass.
A stepstool is needed to look on the upper shelf.
Ticklish skin, as I was saying . . . but his natural impatience
is so profound, that inside his body the parts of his skeleton
behave like pebbles in a torrent!

Seen from the apse, the highest animal nave in the stable . . .

Great saint! Great horse! Beautiful behind in the stable . . .
What is this splendid courtesan's behind that greets me, set
on slim legs, high heels?
Giant goose of the golden eggs, strangely clipped.
Ah, it is the smell of gold that assails my nostrils!
Leather and manure mixed together.
Strong-smelling omelette, from the goose of the golden eggs.
Straw omelette, earth omelette, flavored with the rum of
your urine, dropping from the crack under your tail . . .
As though fresh from the oven, on a pastry sheet, the stable's
rolls and rum balls.

Great saint, with your Byzantine eyes, woeful, under the harness . . .

A sort of saint, humble monk at prayer, in the twilight.

A monk? What am I saying? . . . A pontiff, on his excremental palanquin! A pope—exhibiting to all comers a splendid courtesan's behind, generously heart-shaped, on slender legs ending elegantly in high-heeled shoes.

WHAT IS THIS CLACKING OF THE BIT?

THESE DULL THUDS IN THE STALL?

WHAT'S GOING ON?

PONTIFF AT PRAYER?

SCHOOLBOY IN DETENTION?

GREAT SAINTS! GREAT HORSES (HORSES OR HEROES?), OF THE BEAUTIFUL BEHIND IN THE STABLE,

WHY, SAINTLY MONK, ARE YOU WEARING RIDING BREECHES?

—INTERRUPTED DURING HIS MASS, HE TURNED HIS BYZANTINE EYES TOWARD US . . .

FRANCIS PONGE
translated by Beth Archer

What fall amounts to is really a cold infusion. The dead
leaves of all herb species steep in the rain. But no fermenting
goes on, no alcohol-making: one has to wait until spring to
see the effect a compress has when applied to a
wooden leg.

The counting of votes goes on chaotically. All the doors of the
polling places fly open and slam shut. Into the wastebasket! Into
the wastebasket! Nature rips up her manuscripts, tears down
her bookcases, knocks down the last fruits with long poles.

Then she rises crisply from her work table. Her height all at
once seems unusual. Her hair undone, she has her head in the fog.
Arms loose, she breathes in with ecstasy the icy wind that
makes all her ideas clear. The days are short, the night falls swiftly,
who needs comedy.

Earth floating among the other planets regains her serious
look. Her sunlit side is smaller, invaded by clefts of shadow.
Her shoes, like a hobo's, are great with water, and a source
of music.

Inside this frogpond, or energetic amphibiousness, everything
regains strength, hops from stone to stone, tries a new field.
Streams increase.

Here you see what is called a real soaking, a cleaning that
cares nothing for respectability! Dressed as a naked man, soaked
to the bone.

And it goes on, doesn't get dry right away. Three months
of healthy reflecting goes on in this state; without any circulatory
disaster, without bathrobe, without horsehair glove. But her
strong constitution can take it.

And so, when the tiny buds begin to point, they know what
their source is and what is going on—and if they come out
hesitatingly, numb and flushed, it is in full knowledge of why.

Ah well, but there hangs another tale—that may follow from, but certainly doesn't have the smell of, the black wooden ruler which I will use now to draw my line under this present story.

FRANCIS PONGE
translated by Robert Bly

A snake came to my water-trough
On a hot, hot day, and I in pyjamas for the heat,
To drink there.

In the deep, strange-scented shade of the great dark carob-tree
I came down the steps with my pitcher
And must wait, must stand and wait, for there he was at the
    trough before me.

He reached down from a fissure in the earth-wall in the gloom
And trailed his yellow-brown slackness soft-bellied down, over
    the edge of the stone trough
And rested his throat upon the stone bottom,
And where the water had dripped from the tap, in a small
    clearness,
He sipped with his straight mouth,
Softly drank through his straight gums, into his slack long body,
Silently.

Someone was before me at my water-trough,
And I, like a second comer, waiting.

He lifted his head from his drinking, as cattle do,
And looked at me vaguely, as drinking cattle do,
And flickered his two-forked tongue from his lips, and mused
    a moment,
And stooped and drank a little more,
Being earth-brown, earth-golden from the burning bowels of
    the earth
On the day of Sicilian July, with Etna smoking.

The voice of my education said to me
He must be killed,
For in Sicily the black, black snakes are innocent, the gold
    are venomous.

223

And voices in me said, If you were a man
You would take a stick and break him now, and finish him off.

But must I confess how I like him,
How glad I was he had come like a guest in quiet, to drink at
    my water-trough
And depart peaceful, pacified, and thankless,
Into the burning bowels of this earth?

Was it cowardice, that I dared not kill him?
Was it perversity, that I longed to talk to him?
Was it humility, to feel so honoured?
I felt so honoured.

And yet those voices:
If you were not afraid, you would kill him!

And truly I was afraid, I was most afraid,
But even so, honoured still more
That he should seek my hospitality
From out the dark door of the secret earth.

He drank enough
And lifted his head, dreamily, as one who has drunken,
And flickered his tongue like a forked night on the air, so black,
Seeming to lick his lips,
And looked around like a god, unseeing, into the air.
And slowly turned his head,
And slowly, very slowly, as if thrice adream,
Proceeded to draw his slow length curving round
And climb again the broken bank of my well-face.

And as he put his head into that dreadful hole,
And as he slowly drew up, snake-easing his shoulders, and
    entered farther,
A sort of horror, a sort of protest against his withdrawing
    into that horrid black hole,

Deliberately going into the blackness, and slowly drawing
  himself after,
Overcame me now his back was turned.

I looked around, I put down my pitcher,
I picked up a clumsy log
And threw it at the water-trough with a clatter.

I think it did not hit him,
But suddenly that part of him that was left behind convulsed
  in undignified haste,
Writhed like lightning, and was gone
Into the black hole, the earth-lipped fissure in the wall-front,
At which, in the intense still noon, I stared with fascination.

And immediately I regretted it.
I thought how paltry, how vulgar, what a mean act!
I despised myself and the voices of my accursed human education.

And I thought of the albatross,
And I wished he would come back, my snake.

For he seemed to me again like a king,
Like a king in exile, uncrowned in the underworld,
Now due to be crowned again.

And so, I missed my chance with one of the lords
Of life.
And I have something to expiate;
A pettiness.

D. H. LAWRENCE

STUDY OF TWO PEARS

I

Opusculum paedagogum.
The pears are not viols,
Nudes or bottles.
They resemble nothing else.

II

They are yellow forms
Composed of curves
Bulging toward the base.
They are touched red.

III

They are not flat surfaces
Having curved outlines.
They are round
Tapering toward the top.

IV

In the way they are modelled
There are bits of blue.
A hard dry leaf hangs
From the stem.

V

The yellow glistens.
It glistens with various yellows,
Citrons, oranges and greens
Flowering over the skin.

VI

The shadows of the pears
Are blobs on the green cloth.
The pears are not seen
As the observer wills.

WALLACE STEVENS

'We saw reindeer
browsing,' a friend who'd been in Lapland, said:
'finding their own food; they are adapted

to scant *reino*
or pasture, yet they can run eleven
miles in fifty minutes; the feet spread when

the snow is soft,
and act as snow-shoes. They are rigorists,
however handsomely cutwork artists

of Lapland and
Siberia elaborate the trace
or saddle-girth with saw-tooth leather lace.

One looked at us
with its firm face part brown, part white,—a queen
of alpine flowers. Santa Claus' reindeer, seen

at last, had grey-
brown fur, with a neck like edelweiss or
lion's foot,—*leontopodium* more

exactly.' And
this candelabrum-headed ornament
for a place where ornaments are scarce, sent

to Alaska,
was a gift preventing the extinction
of the Esquimo. The battle was won

by a quiet man,
Sheldon Jackson, evangel to that race
whose reprieve he read in the reindeer's face.

MARIANNE MOORE

In June, amid the golden fields,
I saw a groundhog lying dead.
Dead he lay; my senses shook,
And mind outshot our naked frailty.
There lowly in the vigorous summer
His form began its senseless change,
And made my senses waver dim
Seeing nature ferocious in him.
Inspecting close his maggots' might
And seething cauldron of his being,
Half with loathing, half with a strange love,
I poked him with an angry stick.
The fever arose, became a flame
And Vigour circumscribed the skies,
Immense energy in the sun,
And through my frame a sunless trembling.
My stick had done nor good nor harm.
Then stood I silent in the day
Watching the object, as before;
And kept my reverence for knowledge
Trying for control, to be still,
To quell the passion of the blood;
Until I had bent down on my knees
Praying for joy in the sight of decay.
And so I left; and I returned
In Autumn strict of eye, to see
The sap gone out of the groundhog,
But the bony sodden hulk remained.
But the year had lost its meaning,
And in intellectual chains
I lost both love and loathing,
Mured up in the wall of wisdom.

Another summer took the fields again
Massive and burning, full of life,
But when I chanced upon the spot
There was only a little hair left,
And bones bleaching in the sunlight
Beautiful as architecture;
I watched them like a geometer,
And cut a walking stick from a birch.
It has been three years, now.
There is no sign of the groundhog.
I stood there in the whirling summer,
My hand capped a withered heart,
And thought of China and of Greece,
Of Alexander in his tent;
Of Montaigne in his tower,
Of Saint Theresa in her wild lament.

RICHARD EBERHART

The sea wind sways on over the endless oceans—
spreads its wings night and day
rises and sinks again
over the desolate swaying floor of the immortal ocean.
Now it is nearly morning
or it is nearly evening
and the ocean wind feels in its face—the land wind.

Clockbuoys toll morning and evening psalms,
the smoke of a coalboat
or the smoke of a tar-burning phoenician ship fades away at the
    horizons.
The lonely jellyfish who has no history rocks around with
    burning blue feet.
It's nearly evening now or morning.

HARRY MARTINSON
translated by Robert Bly

THE FISH

I caught a tremendous fish
and held him beside the boat
half out of water, with my hook
fast in a corner of his mouth.
He didn't fight.
He hadn't fought at all.
He hung a grunting weight,
battered and venerable
and homely. Here and there
his brown skin hung in strips
like ancient wallpaper,
and its pattern of darker brown
was like wallpaper:
shapes like full-blown roses
stained and lost through age.
He was speckled with barnacles,
fine rosettes of lime,
and infested
with tiny white sea-lice,
and underneath two or three
rags of green weed hung down.
While his gills were breathing in
the terrible oxygen
—the frightening gills,
fresh and crisp with blood,
that can cut so badly—
I thought of the coarse white flesh
packed in like feathers,
the bog bones and the little bones,
the dramatic reds and blacks
of his shiny entrails,
and the pink swim-bladder

like a big peony.
I looked into his eyes
which were far larger than mine
but shallower, and yellowed,
the irises backed and packed
with tarnished tinfoil
seen through the lenses
of old scratched isinglass.
They shifted a little, but not
to return my stare.
—It was more like the tipping
of an object toward the light.
I admired his sullen face,
the mechanism of his jaw,
and then I saw
that from his lower lip
—if you could call it a lip—
grim, wet, and weaponlike,
hung five old pieces of fish-line,
or four and a wire leader
with the swivel still attached,
with all their five big hooks
grown firmly in his mouth.
A green line, frayed at the end
where he broke it, two heavier lines,
and a fine black thread
still crimped from the strain and snap
when it broke and he got away.
Like medals with their ribbons
frayed and wavering,
a five-haired beard of wisdom
trailing from his aching jaw.
I stared and stared
and victory filled up

234

the little rented boat,
from the pool of bilge
where oil had spread a rainbow
around the rusted engine
to the bailer rusted orange,
the sun-cracked thwarts,
the oarlocks on their strings,
the gunnels—until everything
was rainbow, rainbow, rainbow!
And I let the fish go.

ELIZABETH BISHOP

A bat is born
Naked and blind and pale.
His mother makes a pocket of her tail
And catches him. He clings to her long fur
By his thumbs and toes and teeth.
And then the mother dances through the night
Doubling and looping, soaring, somersaulting—
Her baby hangs on underneath.
All night, in happiness, she hunts and flies.
Her high sharp cries
Like shining needlepoints of sound
Go out into the night, and echoing back,
Tell her what they have touched.
She hears how far it is, how big it is,
Which way it's going:
She lives by hearing.
The mother eats the moths and gnats she catches
In full flight; in full flight
The mother drinks the water of the pond
She skims across. Her baby hangs on tight.
Her baby drinks the milk she makes him
In moonlight or starlight, in mid-air.
Their single shadow, printed on the moon
Or fluttering across the stars,
Whirls on all night; at daybreak
The tired mother flaps home to her rafter.
The others all are there.
They hang themselves up by their toes,
They wrap themselves in their brown wings.
Bunched upside-down, they sleep in air.

Their sharp ears, their sharp teeth, their quick sharp faces
Are dull and slow and mild.
All the bright day, as the mother sleeps,
She folds her wings about her sleeping child.

RANDALL JARRELL

1

Walking north toward the point, I come on a dead seal. From a few feet away, he looks like a brown log. He is on his back, dead only a few hours. I stand and look at him. There's a quiver in the dead flesh. My God he's still alive. A shock goes through me, as if a wall of my room had fallen away.

The head is arched back, the small eyes closed, the whiskers sometimes rise and fall. He is dying. This is the oil. Here on its back is the oil that heats our houses so efficiently. Wind blows fine sand back toward the ocean. The flipper near me lies folded over the stomach, looking like an unfinished arm, lightly glazed with sand at the edges. The other flipper lies half underneath. The seal's skin looks like an old overcoat, scratched here and there, by sharp musselshells maybe . . .

So I reach out and touch him. Suddenly he rears up, turns over, gives three cries, Awaaark! Awaaark! Awaaark!—like the cries from Christmas toys. He lunges toward me. I am terrified and leap back, although I know there can be no teeth in that jaw. He starts flopping toward the sea. But he falls over, on his face. He does not want to go back to the sea. He looks up at the sky, and he looks like an old lady who has lost her hair.

He puts his chin back down on the sand, rearranges his flippers, and waits for me to go. I go.

2

Today I go back to say goodbye. He's dead now. But he's not—he's a quarter mile farther up the shore. Today he is thinner, squatting on his stomach, head out. The ribs show more—each vertebra on the back underneath the coat is now visible, shiny. He breathes in and out.

He raises himself up, and tucks his flippers under, as if to keep them warm. A wave comes in, touches his nose. He turns and looks at me—the eyes slanted, the crown of his head looks like a boy's leather jacket bending over his bicycle bars. He is taking a long time to die. The whiskers white as porcupine quills, the forehead slopes . . . goodbye brother, die in the sound of waves, forgive us if we have killed you, long live your race, your inner-tube race, so uncomfortable on land, so comfortable in the ocean. Be comfortable in death then, when the sand will be out of your nostrils, and you can swim in long loops through the pure death, ducking under as assassinations break above you. You don't want to be touched by me. I climb the cliff and go home the other way.

ROBERT BLY

I saw the salt
in this shaker
in the salt flats.
I know
you
will never believe me,
but
it sings,
the salt sings, the hide
of the salt plains,
it sings
through a mouth smothered
by earth.
I shuddered in those deep
solitudes
when I heard
the voice
of
the salt
in the desert.
Near Antofagasta
the entire
salt plain
speaks:
it is a
broken
voice,
a song full
of grief.
Then in its own mines
rock salt, a mountain
of buried light,
a cathedral through which light passes,

crystal of the sea, abandoned
by the waves.

And then on every table
on this earth, ⌐ in the world,
salt,
your nimble
body
pouring out
the vigorous light
over
our foods.
Preserver
of the stores
on the ancient ships,
you were
an explorer
in the ocean,
substance
going first
over the unknown, barely open
routes of the sea-foam.
Dust of the sea, the tongue
receives a kiss
of the night sea from you:
taste recognizes
the ocean in each salted morsel,
and therefore the smallest,
the tiniest
wave of the shaker
brings home to us
not only your domestic whiteness
but the inward flavor of the infinite.

PABLO NERUDA
translated by Robert Bly

The tree of intense
summer,
hard,
is all blue sky,
yellow sun,
fatigue in drops,
a sword
above the highways,
a scorched shoe
in the cities:
the brightness and the world
weigh us down,
hit us
in the eyes
with clouds of dust,
with sudden golden blows,
they torture
our feet
with tiny thorns,
with hot stones,
and the mouth
suffers
more than all the toes:
the throat
becomes thirsty,
the teeth,
the lips, the tongue:
we want to drink
waterfalls,
the dark blue night,
the South Pole,
and then

the coolest of all
the planets crosses
the sky,
the round, magnificent,
star-filled watermelon.

It's a fruit from the thirst-tree.
It's the green whale of the summer.

The dry universe
all at once
given dark stars
by this firmament of coolness
lets the swelling
fruit
come down:
its hemispheres open
showing a flag
green, white, red,
that dissolves into
wild rivers, sugar,
delight!

Jewel box of water, phlegmatic
queen
of the fruitshops,
warehouse
of profundity, moon
on earth!
You are pure,
rubies fall apart
in your abundance,
and we
want
to bite into you.

to bury our
face
in you, and
our hair, and
the soul!
When we're thirsty
we glimpse you
like
a mine or a mountain
of fantastic food,
but
among our longings and our teeth
you change
simply
into cool light
that slips in turn into
spring water
that touched us once
singing.
And that is why
you don't weigh us down
in the siesta hour
that's like an oven,
you don't weigh us down,
you just
go by
and your heart, some cold ember,
turned itself into a single
drop of water.

PABLO NERUDA
translated by Robert Bly

ARCHAIC TORSO OF APOLLO

We have no idea what his fantastic head
was like, where the eyeballs were slowly swelling. But
his body now is glowing like a lamp
whose inner eyes, only turned down a little,

hold their flame, shine. If there weren't light, the curve
of the breast wouldn't blind you, and in the swerve
of the thighs a smile wouldn't keep on going
toward the place where the seeds are.

If there weren't light, this stone would look cut off
where it drops so clearly from the shoulders,
its skin wouldn't gleam like the fur of a wild animal,

and the body wouldn't send out light from every edge
as a star does . . . for there is no place at all
that isn't looking at you. You must change your life.

RAINER MARIA RILKE
translated by Robert Bly

THE PANTHER

Jardin des Plantes, Paris

From seeing and seeing the seeing has become so exhausted
it no longer sees anything anymore.
The world is made of bars, a hundred thousand
bars, and behind the bars, nothing.

The lithe swinging of that rhythmical easy stride
that slowly circles down to a single point
is like a dance of energy around a hub,
in which a great will stands stunned and numbed.

At times the curtains of the eye lift
without a sound—then a shape enters,
slips through the tightened silence of the shoulders,
reaches the heart and dies.

RAINER MARIA RILKE
translated by Robert Bly

Palm of the hand. Sole that walks now
only on feeling. It turns over,
becomes a mirror,
shows sky roads, which
themselves are walking.
It has learned to walk on water,
when it dips down,
moves on springs,
causes all roads to fork.
Comes forward into other palms,
those like itself
turn into a countryside,
through them it travels and arrives,
fills them with having arrived.

RAINER MARIA RILKE
translated by Robert Bly

STONE

Go inside a stone.
That would be my way.
Let somebody else become a dove
Or gnash with a tiger's tooth.
I am happy to be a stone.

From the outside the stone is a riddle:
No one knows how to answer it.
Yet within, it must be cool and quiet
Even though a cow steps on it full weight,
Even though a child throws it in a river;
The stone sinks, slow, unperturbed
To the river bottom
Where the fishes come to knock on it
And listen.

I have seen sparks fly out
When two stones are rubbed,
So perhaps it is not dark inside after all;
Perhaps there is a moon shining
From somewhere, as though behind a hill—
Just enough light to make out
The strange writings, the star-charts
On the inner walls.

CHARLES SIMIC

Part six:
Leaving the house

Sometimes I go about pitying myself,
and all the time
I am being carried on great winds across the sky.

Ojibway
adapted by Robert Bly
from the translation of Frances Densmore

THIS book asks one question over and over: how much consciousness is the poet willing to grant to trees or hills or living creatures not a part of his own species? I think it is possible to say that every city culture, sooner or later, develops its Descartes; I mean a thinker who encourages the gap the citizen already feels between himself and nature. When the gap develops, the human being changes. The change shows itself practically in an emphasis on perception—what Kant calls the noumena—rather than on the object that has drawn forth the perception. Rather than working to describe a sea urchin, people prefer to say, "The sea urchin is beautiful," or "The sea urchin is ugly." Because of the human being's hugging of his own perceptions, which Descartes' ideas encourage, the energy, both sexual and spiritual, tends to become interiorized inside the body. It circulates "harmlessly" inside the human body, and does not leave it. Rilke in an early poem describes this locked-in situation well, using the metaphor of house-bonding.

> Whoever you are: some evening take a step
> out of your house, which you know so well.
> Enormous space is near, your house lies where it begins,
> whoever you are.
> Your eyes find it hard to tear themselves
> from the sloping threshold, but with your eyes

slowly, slowly, lift one black tree
up, so it stands against the sky: skinny, alone.
With that you have made the world. The world is immense,
and like a word that is still growing in the silence.
In the same moment that your will grasps it,
your eyes feeling its subtlety will leave it. . . .

Rilke says clearly that the problem is to "leave the house." But
human beings are eaters of consciousness, hungry for it; why leave
the house if you're convinced there is consciousness only inside
your house, or inside your own species? Rilke's poem says that if
you make the effort to use your entire imaginative power to see
one tree, you've essentially granted the whole world its being.
Giving yourself to that one tree is crucial.

Rilke in this poem is describing a practical way to heal the
Descartes wound; it involves imaginative labor, and that labor
cannot be done by the collective. Each person has to do it alone.
I'm not sure, but I think it is a fair guess that there are some cultures
in which a person does not have to do that by will, because a
Descartes has not yet come. I would guess that the Eskimos of the
last century, whom Rasmussen visited, belonged to such a culture.
The short poem an Eskimo woman shaman spoke to Rasmussen,
which I've called "The Great Sea," lives where the outer world
flows naturally into the intestines and stomach. Poor Wolf tells of
his odd experience with the bear when he was seventeen, and the
bear entered his teepee as naturally as the ocean entered the Es-
kimo woman's stomach. What touches me most in his account are
the things he kept near him after that incident. He knew it was an
important meeting. "I had a dried turtle skull, a mink skin, red
muscles, a crane's head, an otter skin—six things, besides pepper-
mint and other herbs." Later he paid with his own considerable
labor, for he no doubt decorated the buffalo skins himself, for "a
bear's arm, a crane's head, an owl's head, a buffalo skull, and a
sweet-grass braid that represented a snake with two heads."

In the Zuni poem, the person speaking, who I believe is a
woman, declares that only if her energy leaves her body can the

prayer for a heavy winter be effective; and the test of that is whether the "prayer sticks" come alive or just remain sticks.

I suspect *Beowulf* was written in this same cultural milieu, the milieu before Descartes, in which the speaker has faith in night-time events. I've chosen one passage from *Beowulf*. A writer, rather than saying abstractly, "There is a consciousness out there so real it is dangerous," can say instead: "Once there was a being named Grendel." Burton Raffel's translation suggests the terrific energy which the sound and images of the original Anglo-Saxon poem give to that being. Such a complete granting seems beyond any Western poet at the moment. If he or she did feel the consciousness, so much awareness of sound has been lost in the last two thousand years that it would be difficult for him to grant it. Among English and Scottish ballads composed a few centuries after *Beowulf*, the sound patterns, though they became more conventional, and even collectivized, in comparison with the oceanic feeling of *Beowulf*, continued to carry into the minds of all who heard them the awareness of the power of night events. A writer can say: "There is a consciousness out there so powerful it is dangerous," or he can say, "I knew a woman once who got stolen by a weird creature." To call it a demon lover is not quite right, since it is neither a demon nor a lover. But we know it is something.

"The Falcon" is such a mysterious poem. It is definitely Christian, and yet it continues the abduction theme. The theme of it is "The falcon has carried my mate away."

Lully, lulley, lully, lulley!
The fawcon hath born my make away!

He bare hym up, he bare hym down,
He bare hym into an orchard brown.

In that orchard there was an halle
That was hangid with purpill and pall.

And yn that hall there was a bede,
Hit was hangid with gold so rede.

And yn that bed there lythe a knyght,
His woundis bledyng day and nyght.

By that bedeside kneleth a may,
And she wepeth both nyght and day.

And by that bedeside there stondith a ston,
'Corpus Christi' wretyn theron.

Lully, lulley, lully, lulley!
The fawcon hath born my make away!

The poem implies that the ego has been captured by forces ex-
tremely powerful, associated with wild nature, or a nature only
partially tamed, for which the falcon can well stand.

As we read, a strange scene unfolds: the person watching wit-
nesses the non-human energy carry the "mate" part of the per-
sonality to an orchard-room. The orchard room has the mood of
grief, and something, called here a knight, is lying on a bed
wounded. The knight is open, but in the wrong way, so that energy
runs out of him night and day. The leaving weakens the knight.
The poem seems to say that when the gap has been opened, the
personality experiences tremendous suffering. Freud made that
suffering the first principle of his work, as Buddha had done
earlier. During the Middle Ages, Western poems began to empha-
size not the Grendel consciousness that controls the nighttime
events, and abducts the ego, but instead the suffering of the human
being who is locked in his room, bleeding to death. In this room a
woman weeps near him. That the room is inside an orchard, a place
of fruitfulness, doesn't decrease the loss or the fear. The person
who composed "The Falcon" makes at this point a wonderful
leap. He guesses that the desperate situation of the knight, unable
to fight Grendel's mother or buy an owl's head, is somehow asso-
ciated with "corpus christi," the body of Christ," which has
turned into a stone. We remember that Faithful John's body, in the
German fairy tale collected by the Brothers Grimm, also turned
to stone; in fact, Faithful John, turned entirely to stone, stood for

years in the bedroom of the King and Queen. "The Falcon" seems to say that when the knight becomes locked inside his own room, then the body of Christ turns to stone. The orchard room then contains four beings: the watcher, the wounded knight, the sobbing woman, and the stone representing Christ. The author of the poem does not know, or at least say, how to turn the stone back again to living flesh. By contrast, whoever composed "Faithful John" describes toward the close of the tale how the King and Queen eventually got the stone out of their bedroom and turned back into a living person. Presumably the bleeding also stops then. Surely this attempt to turn stone to flesh is what Freud and Jung have tried to do.

I think one could say that the Faithful John part of Rilke's psyche has come alive, and that Faithful John is alive also in Francis Ponge's psyche. Rilke's lifework and Ponge's lifework suggest that attention to the object leads after many years to stone coming alive again, and so to a new unity of the "King" and "Queen." The unity of the personality is a garden, or orchard. Rumi refuses to describe it abstractly. He says:

> How marvellous is that garden, where apples and pears, both for the
>   sake of the two Marys,
> are arriving even in winter.
>
> Those apples grow from the Gift, and sink back into the Gift.
> It must be that they are coming from the garden to the garden.

So ecology contains in it a secret, over and above its scientific and its political meaning. The renewed attention to the panther and the tree in our culture is something to rejoice over. As David Ignatow has remarked, looking at things puts one in the mood to praise. Rilke, in the seventh "Sonnet to Orpheus" says

> To praise in the whole thing. A man who can praise
> comes toward us like ore out of the silences
> of rock. His heart, that dies, presses out
> for others a wine that is fresh forever.

254

When the god's image takes hold of him,
his voice never collapses in the dust.
Everything turns to vineyards, everything turns to grapes,
made ready for harvest by his powerful south.

The mold in the catacomb of the king
does not suggest that his praising is lies, nor
the fact that the gods cast shadows.

He is one of the servants who does not go away,
who still holds through the doors
of the tomb trays of shining fruit.

I have put into this section a few poems that feel "whole,"
"healed," from widely separated cultures, just to see what our
poetry may look like in a couple of hundred years. One notices that
the American Indian poems and Eskimo poems have curious links
with the poems "of high culture" written by Rumi, Kabir and
Mirabai, as well as with the poetry of the contemporary Zen
meditator, Shinkichi Takahashi. If we use the image offered by the
person who composed "The Falcon," Poor Wolf's poem takes
place before the knight begins to bleed, Mirabai and Takahashi's
poems take place after the healing has begun. That schemata is far
too simplistic, because the bleeding and the healing surely take
place in every instant of time, in every culture, and always have,
even before human beings were born, but it's a way of talking.
Everything I have said is just a way of talking.

I would say that Kabir has gone through a long process of private
suffering that happened before the poems that we know of ap-
peared. He was abducted and returned. He followed a road
through the object until he found himself in a field where the ob-
ject is not a symbol. After his abduction and return, Kabir has the
confidence in Poem 37 to say of a "spiritual athlete":

Or he sits inside a shrine room all day,
so that God has to go out and praise the rocks.

Speaking of his body, he says:

Inside this clay jug there are canyons and pine mountains,
and the maker of canyons and pine mountains.
All seven oceans are inside, and hundreds of millions of stars.

Bashō, after a long struggle, probably lasting twenty or thirty years, arrived at a point where his poems were neither subjective nor objective. Two examples might be:

The temple bell stops.
But the sound keeps coming
out of the flowers.

Another:

It's late on in fall.
I walked around the shore
of the lake all night!

Takahashi, in a fraction of a second, switches, nine or ten times inside each poem, from the inner to the outer, until they are stitched together.

Mirabai's poems are perhaps the most astonishing of all. She writes mainly of Krishna, whose body is imagined as dark blue or violet in color. She has traveled for thousands of miles along the road that Ponge follows, and, speaking of Krishna, she says:

Without the energy that lifts mountains, how am I to live?

In her confidence, self-pity leaves:

The energy that holds up mountains is the energy Mirabai bows down to.
He lives century after century, and the test I set for him he has passed.

Anything more I could say about Mirabai the reader, after reading her poems, would already understand. With Mirabai, we have come a long way from the poetry of condescension.

THE GREAT SEA

The great sea
Has sent me adrift,
It moves me as the weed in a great river,
Earth and the great weather move me,
Have carried me away,
And move my inward parts with joy.

ESKIMO WOMAN SHAMAN
quoted by Rasmussen

In the very earliest time,
when both people and animals lived on earth,
a person could become an animal if he wanted to
and an animal could become a human being.
Sometimes they were people
and sometimes animals
and there was no difference.
All spoke the same language.
That was the time when words were like magic.
The human mind had mysterious powers.
A word spoken by chance
might have strange consequences.
It would suddenly come alive
and what people wanted to happen could happen—
all you had to do was say it.
Nobody can explain this:
That's the way it was.

after NALUNGIAQ

When I was a child of five winters, perhaps only four, I prayed to the spirits of animals, to the stars, the sun and the moon. My words were not many, but I prayed. I was afraid of the enemy in the dark. My father had heard of the white man's God through a trader but nothing clearly. We sometimes prayed to the white man's God who made us and could make us grow.

We had female divinities above, and we prayed to the four winds, and to the earth that makes the corn grow. There are many songs concerning these things, some of the songs speak of the different colored flowers. These things were taught for a great price, by the priests of the tribe.

⊠   ⊠   ⊠

When I was seventeen years of age I had the small pox. I was left alone in a lodge, helpless, weak, and my eyes nearly closed. A bear came in and walked up to where I was lying. He sat down with his back pressed against me, and began to scratch his breast with his fore paws. By and by he got up and walked out of the lodge. Was I dreaming or had it really happened? While I was thinking it over the bear returned, and while I trembled for fear, went through the same motions again, and then went off, leaving me unharmed. I thought surely the bear has had mercy on me. When my father came again we talked it over and agreed that the bear had pitied me. After that I worshipped the bear, and in the dance I wore anklets of bear's teeth.

⊠   ⊠   ⊠

I had a dried turtle shell, a muskrat skin, a mink skin, red muscles, a crane's head, an otter skin—six things, besides peppermint and other herbs. For these, and the songs and so forth connected with them, I paid eighty buffalo hides, besides

259

guns, ponies, etc. I keep the turtle shell and the muscles yet, because they belong to my father; but I do not worship them. At one time, I paid one hundred and eighty buffalo hides, ten of which were decorated with porcupine work, and knives, and ponies, for a bear's arm, a crane's head, an owl's head, a buffalo skull, and a sweet-grass braid that represented a snake with two heads. There were other things. The long hair of the buffalo near the jaw, owl's claws, and an image of an owl in buffalo hair. Such things were used at the buffalo dance for conjuring. These things give the strength of the buffalo in fighting with the enemy. They also bring the buffalo when food is scarce. They also cure wounds. There is also corn in the ear, and in a basket; red foxes, swift foxes, arrow heads, and things to make the wind blow right. Such things as these I took out on to a hill, talked to them, saying I do not need you any more, and threw them to the winds. For doing so Crow Breast, the Gros Ventre chief, called me a fool.

POOR WOLF (GROS VENTRE)

OFFERING

This is what I want to happen: that our earth mother
may be clothed in ground corn four times over;
that frost flowers cover her over entirely;
that the mountain pines far away over there
may stand close to each other in the cold;
that the weight of snow crack some branches!
In order that the country may be this way
I have made my prayer sticks into something alive.

ZUNI
adapted by Robert Bly from the
translation by Ruth Bunzel

FOOT RACE SONG

Many people have gathered together,
   I am ready to start in the race,
And the Swallow with beating wings
   Cools me in readiness for the word.

Far in the west the black mountain stands
   Around which our racers run at noon.
Who is this man running with me,
   The shadow of whose hands I see?

PIMA
translated by Frank Russell

. . . They named the huge one Grendel:
If he had a father no one knew him,
Or whether there'd been others before these two,
Hidden evil before hidden evil.
They live in secret places, windy
Cliffs, wolf-dens where water pours
From the rocks, then runs underground, where mist
Steams like black clouds, and the groves of trees
Growing out over their lake are all covered
With frozen spray, and wind down snakelike
Roots that reach as far as the water
And help keep it dark. At night that lake
Burns like a torch. No one knows its bottom,
No wisdom reaches such depths. A deer,
Hunted through the woods by packs of hounds,
A stag with great horns, though driven through the forest
From faraway places, prefers to die
On those shores, refuses to save its life
In that water. It isn't far, nor is it
A pleasant spot! When the wind stirs
And storms, waves splash toward the sky,
As dark as the air, as black as the rain
That the heavens weep . . .

from *Beowulf*
translated by Burton Raffel

"O where have you been, my long, long love,
　This long seven years and mair?"
"O I'm come to seek my former vows
　Ye granted me before."

"O hold your tongue of your former vows,
　For they will breed sad strife;
O hold your tongue of your former vows,
　For I am become a wife."

He turned him right and round about,
　And the tear blinded his ee:
"I wad never hae trodden on Irish ground
　If it had not been for thee.

"I might hae had a king's daughter,
　Far, far beyond the sea;
I might have had a king's daughter,
　Had it not been for love o thee."

"If ye might have had a king's daughter,
　Yersel ye had to blame;
Ye might have taken the king's daughter,
　For ye kend that I was nane.

"If I was to leave my husband dear,
　And my two babes also,
O what have you to take me to,
　If with you I should go?"

"I hae seven ships upon the sea—
　The eighth brought me to land—

With four-and-twenty bold mariners,
    And music on every hand."

She has taken up her two little babes,
    Kissed them baith cheek and chin:
"O fair ye weel, my ain two babes,
    For I'll never see you again."

She set her foot upon the ship,
    No mariners could she behold;
But the sails were of the taffetie,
    And the masts of the beaten gold.

She had not sailed a league, a league,
    A league but barely three,
When dismal grew his countenance,
    And drumlie grew his ee.

They had not saild a league, league,
    A league but barely three,
Until she espied his cloven foot,
    And she wept right bitterlie.

"O hold your tongue of your weeping," says he,
    "Of your weeping now let me be;
I will shew you how the lilies grow
    On the banks of Italy."

"O what hills are yon, yon pleasant hills,
    That the sun shines sweetly on?"
"O yon are the hills of heaven," he said,
    "Where you will never win."

"O whaten a mountain is yon," she said,
    All so dreary wi frost and snow?"

"O yon is the mountain of hell," he cried,
   "Where you and I will go."

He strack the tap-mast wi his hand,
   The fore-mast wi his knee,
And he brake that gallant ship in twain,
   And sank her in the sea.

ANONYMOUS
England and Scotland,
perhaps Middle Ages or earlier

Lully, lulley, lully, lulley!
The fawcon hath born my make away!

He bare hym up, he bare hym down,
He bare hym into an orchard brown.

In that orchard there was an halle
That was hangid with purpill and pall.

And yn that hall there was a bede,
Hit was hangid with gold so rede.

And yn that bed there lythe a knyght,
His woundis bledyng day and nyght.

By that bedeside kneleth a may,
And she wepeth both nyght and day.

And by that bedeside there stondith a ston,
'Corpus Christi' wretyn thereon.

Lully, lulley, lully, lulley!
The fawcon hath born my make away!

England, perhaps thirteenth century

You should try to hear the name the Holy One has for things.
There is something in the phrase: "The Holy One has taught
   him names."
We name every thing according to the number of legs it has;
the other one names it according to what it has inside.
Moses waved his stick; he thought it was a "rod,"
but inside its name was "dragonish snake."
We thought the name of Blake was "agitator against priests,"
but in eternity his name is "the one who believes."
No one knows our name until our last breath goes out.

RUMI
version by Robert Bly

The drunkards are rolling in slowly, those who hold to wine
    are approaching.
The lovers come, singing, from the garden, the ones with
    brilliant eyes.

The I-don't-want-to-lives are leaving, and the I-want-to-lives
    are arriving.
They have gold sewn into their clothes, sewn in for those who
    have none.

Those with ribs showing who have been grazing in the old
    pasture of love
are turning up fat and frisky.

The souls of pure teachers are arriving like rays of sunlight
from so far up to the ground-huggers.

How marvellous is that garden, where apples and pears, both
    for the sake of the two Marys,
are arriving even in winter.

Those apples grow from the Gift, and sink back into the Gift.
It must be that they are coming from the garden to the garden.

RUMI
version by Robert Bly

1

I built my hut near where people live
and yet I hear no traffic noise or sound of wheels.
Could you tell me what is happening?
An aloneness gathers around the soul that is alone.
I pick chrysanthemums underneath the east hedge,
the mountains to the south are clear.
The mountain air at sunset is so wonderful,
and the birds coming home, one after the other.
In all these details there are secret truths;
but when I try to shift to language, it all slips away.

2

Such a strong color on the late chrysanthemums!
The stalk sways stoutly, flower wet with dew, open.
Wandering drunk in this beauty, who cares about my sorrows.
I have left excitement behind, and what is not done.
Alone, I take a drink.
The bottle tilts by itself when the cup is empty.
When the sun goes down, all bustle stops,
and the birds on their return call from the leaves.
I walk around my study shouting and proud
because I can take up this life again.

TAO YUAN-MING
adapted by Robert Bly from the
translation of Marjorie Sinclair

Student, do the simple purification.

You know that the seed is inside the horse-chestnut tree,
and inside the seed there are the horse-chestnut blossoms, and
    the chestnuts, and the shade.
So inside the human body there is the seed, and inside the seed
    there is the human body again.

Fire, air, earth, water, and space—if you don't want the secret
    one,
you can't have these either.

Thinkers, listen, tell me what you know of that is not inside
    the soul?
Take a pitcher full of water and set it down on the water—
now it has water inside and water outside.
We mustn't give it a name, lest silly people start talking
    again about the body and the soul.

If you want the truth, I'll tell you the truth:
Listen to the secret sound, the real sound, which is inside you.
The one no one talks of speaks the secret sound to himself,
and he's the one who has made it all.

KABIR
version by Robert Bly

271

Inside this clay jug there are canyons and pine mountains,
and the maker of canyons and pine mountains!
All seven oceans are inside, and hundreds of millions of stars.
The acid that tests gold is there, and the one who judges jewels.
And the music from the strings that no one touches, and the
   source of all water.

If you want the truth, I will tell you the truth:
Friend, listen: the God whom I love is inside.

KABIR
version by Robert Bly

FISH

I hold a newspaper, reading.
Suddenly my hands become cow ears,
They turn into Pusan, the South Korean port.

Lying on a mat
Spread on the bankside stones,
I fell asleep.
But a willow leaf, breeze stirred,
Brushed my ear.
I remained just as I was,
Near the murmurous water.

When young there was a girl
Who became a fish for me.
Whenever I wanted fish
Broiled in salt, I'd summon her.
She'd get down on her stomach
To be sun-cooked on the stones.
And she was always ready!

Alas, she no longer comes to me.
And old benighted drake,
I hobble homeward.
But look, my drake feet become horse hoofs!
Now they drop off
And, stretching marvellously
Become the tracks of the Tōkaido Railway Line.

SHINKICHI TAKAHASHI
translated by Lucien Stryk

SNAIL

The snail crawls over blackness.

Just now, in the garden,
A solid lump of snow
Slipped from the zinc roof
To behead the nandin.

Make it snappy!

In full view a stalk has been
Torn off:
Let the wind rage over the earth,
He is unaware.

His head flies to the end
Of the world,
His body is tossed
Into the ash can.

Could it be that he's the falling snow?

SHINKICHI TAKAHASHI
translated by Lucien Stryk and Takashi Ikemoto

Breastdown fluttering in the breeze,
The sparrow's full of air holes.
Let the winds of winter blow,
Let them crack a wing, two,
The sparrow doesn't care.

The air streams through him, free, easy,
Scattering feathers, bending legs.
He hops calmly, from branch to empty branch
In an absolutely spaceless world.

I'd catch, skewer, broil you,
But my every shot misses: you're impossible.
All at once there's the sound
Of breaking glass, and houses begin
To crumple. Rising quickly,
An atomic submarine nudges past your belly.

SHINKICHI TAKAHASHI
translated by Lucien Stryk and Takashi Ikemoto

When I saw the dark clouds, I wept, Oh Dark One, I wept at
the dark clouds.
Black clouds soared up, and took some yellow along; rain did
fall, some rain fell long.
There was water east of the house, west of the house, fields
all green.
The one I love lives past those fields.
Rain has fallen on my body, on my hair, as I wait in the open
door for him.
The energy that holds up mountains is the one Mirabai bows
down to.
He lives century after century, and the test I set for him he
has passed.

MIRABAI
version by Robert Bly

The colors of the Dark One have penetrated Mira's body;
    other colors washed out.
Making love with Krishna and eating little—those are my
    pearls and my carnelians.
Chanting-beads and the forehead streak—those are my
    bracelets.
That's enough feminine wiles for me. My teacher taught me this.
Approve me or disapprove me; I praise the Mountain Energy
    night and day.
I take the path that ecstatic human beings have taken for
    centuries.
I don't steal money, nor hit anyone; what will you charge me with?
I have felt the swaying of the elephant's shoulders. . . .
    and now you want me to climb on a jackass? Try to be serious!

MIRABAI
version by Robert Bly

Two meditations
as an afterword

A Meditation on a Poem by Goethe

I

THE PSYCHOANALYST Georg Groddeck, in an essay called "Cha-rakter und Typus," written about 1907, gives Goethe as a supreme example of a writer, relatively new to Europe, who brings us "news of the universe." He quotes Goethe's short poem, "Wanderers Nachtlied II":

> *Über allen Gipfeln*
> *Ist Ruh,*
> *In allen Wipfeln*
> *Spürest du*
> *Kaum einen Hauch:*
> *Die Vögelein schweigen im Walde.*
> *Warte nur! Balde*
> *Ruhest du auch.*

In an inadequate English translation, without most of the sound, it reads:

> *There is a stillness*
> *On the tops of the hills.*
> *In the tree tops*
> *You feel*
> *Hardly a breath of air.*
> *The small birds fall silent in the trees.*
> *Simply wait: soon*
> *You too will be silent.*

In historical time we notice that the poem takes place after the discovery by the Romantics that the Alps are beautiful. Goethe is sending his energy, or it is being pulled out of him by the hills at evening. The poem contains an experience many people have had:

280

each time a human being's desire-energy leaves his body, and goes out into the hills or forest, the desire-energy whispers to the ear as it leaves: "You know, one day you will die." I think both men and women need this whisper; it helps the human to come down, to be on the ground. When that whisper comes, it means that the tree-consciousness, the one in the wooded hill, and the one in the man, have spoken to each other. The human being grows sad then, knowing that he or she is an animal who will die.

Groddeck remarks that "Goethe's short poems have a strange ring to them. They are entirely impersonal; in fact, you could say of them that they are not created by a person, but by nature. In them a person is not seen as an 'I,' but as a part of something else." Groddeck makes a strong distinction between the "I" poet, who brings us "news of the human mind" and another sort of poet, who brings "news of the universe." The "I" poets, sometimes classical, sometimes not, speak from the three accepted faculties: feeling, will and intellect. The poets of the other group speak from these faculties also, and are aware of an additional energy inside themselves. Groddeck calls this energy—or whatever it is—*Gott-natur*, which means 'divine instinctuality' from one point of view, but also 'non-human nature.' The Gott-natur senses the inter- dependence of all things alive, and longs to bring them all inside a work of art. We can describe the work of a number of poets—I think especially of Novalis, Goethe, Bashō, Mirabai—as an elab- orate expression of the Gott-natur. A non-human instinctuality helps to shape the poem.

he believes

2

After making his distinction between the two contrasting poetries, Groddeck makes some historical speculations. Groddeck believes that European literature after 1600 or so gradually be- came engrossed in aggressively studying human reactions. He mentions Shakespeare particularly as a leader in the exclusive study of "the human." The Greek dramatists, by contrast, through masks and inclusion of seasonal ritual, brought in much material not directly related to the human. His view of Shakespeare was disturbing to me. He is not denying that Shakespeare is a great writer, but he is saying that Shakespeare provided a model for a literature that ultimately proved narrowing, in that it regarded the "I" as something independent, and threw itself into elaborating its turns and impulses.

Groddeck thought that we are now experiencing, without being able to distinguish them, two separate literatures, one ending, one beginning. The dominant literature, now weakening, is the literature that aggressively studies human reactions. He mentions Pope, Kleist, Byron, and the domestic dramas of Ibsen and Shaw. Ibsen took the middle-class living room up on stage with no changes, because for most of his life he refused to study anything except the human. Groddeck says that this tradition became bankrupt in the nineteenth century, though most writers continued in it without realizing it was <u>bankrupt</u>. European drama, poetry, fiction, music and painting had by 1900, he says, driven themselves into a dead end. I think that *Ulysses*, as well as most modernist painting, belongs to this dead-end art. In fiction, Conrad is an exception. Conrad takes us inside a human mind, but when we get there it turns out we are deep inside a continent. We feel the immensity of nature, how much of it is beyond the ego. "Once, I remember, we came upon a man-of-war, anchored off the coast . . . the muzzles of the long six-inch guns stuck out all over the low hull. . . . In the empty immensity of earth, sky, and water, there she was, incomprehensible, firing into a continent." Conrad is not analyzing his neighbor, he is trying to get some understanding of the interdependence of all the things in the world.

3

Our view in the United States of the modern movement is confused because we have not tried hard enough to distinguish between works which, though impressive, are products of the dying tradition and half dead themselves, and those works that come into being as a fresh start, as a part of the tradition Groddeck saw flowing out of the small poems of Goethe. (It's clear that many of Goethe's longer works belong to the sentimental and extreme pole, so his work contains both streams.)

Groddeck suggests that the word "extreme" is a key to what happens when a culture is unable to break away from "the human." Its writers will be extreme.

> They write of what is out of the ordinary, they make their art from extreme mental states. This is of course quite understandable. Only a person with really sluggish blood could put up with the average interior state of the human being without yawning, and to make art out of it is impossible, at least not in the way Shakespeare and Beethoven go about it. . . . The only poet who could make anything out of it is a man who sees in human beings a part of the universe, for whom human nature is interesting not because it is human, but because it is nature. Goethe could do that, Bach also. However, if an artist has no Gott-natur in him—and one finds this nature these days most often in men who are intellectually silent, very seldom in those who have gone through schools—then he has no choice but to buckle knee-length buskins on his characters. By doing that he makes them more appealing. In other words, he has to look for something extreme; and if it isn't there, he will insert it into his characters by force: he has to be romantic.

And I guess he is right. If a writer is bringing news of the human mind, and he feels that much of the news has been told, then what? Then he will have to bring more extreme news. This news must be sensational, to catch our interest. The writer may gather material for it by making his life extreme: breakdown, rage, madness, suicide. He will not really do it for material, but the literary longing for the extreme may affect his life.

Groddeck is not saying that writers who look for the extreme and find it are bad poets. He's not saying that at all. He is saying that some of our greatest talents and intelligences have become caught in a dying stream, and thresh about in it, suffering, as a large fish in the Platte River. For the extreme poet, anything less than a disaster doesn't justify the poetic machinery. A poem becomes a tank that can't maneuver on soft ground without ruining it. And American readers, becoming coarsened by extreme art—

murders on television—mistake the tank marks on grass for evi-
dence of inner strength, and encourage the poet to be more
extreme, to have another breakdown.

At the same time there is something a little simple-minded about
Groddeck's scheme. I like his bravery in thinking through literary
history himself, and his daring in lumping Shakespeare with the
motorcycle riders. And I think his distinction between two types
of poetry is sound. Yet I am not convinced by his dismissal of all
extreme states of mind. I am not prepared to give up all extreme
art, and have it replaced by short poems. I have struggled hard to
write poems that belong in the tradition of "Wanderers Nacht-
lied," but "The Teeth Mother Naked At Last" is clearly a poetry
of extreme states of mind. I don't think the Vietnam War can be
understood if we try to get rid of our extreme states of mind.

4

I'm going to return to Fascism once more, because it has made
its most violent appearance so far in Germany, and I have praised
much German poetry here. Obviously anything I say can hardly
begin to touch this enormous issue of Fascism, and what it is. With
which of the two traditions—the path of the extreme artists,
glorifying extreme states of mind, or the path of the Gott-natur—
should we associate Fascism? Both and neither. The Nuremberg
rallies showed a mad longing for extreme states of mind, but I don't
believe this means that the extreme artist paves the way for
Nuremberg. Neither is the Nuremberg rally a continuation of the
Novalis night-intelligence, or Goethe's feeling, because the Fas-
cists are even less willing to share consciousness than the Car-
tesians. In general the Fascists hate everything that is weak, which
they believe includes animals and landscape.

Gérard de Nerval is also talking to Hitler's planners when he
says:

> When you gather to plan, the universe is not there.

I think that the Westerner, after centuries of planning—successful
planning—loses touch with nature so much that he loses touch

with her dark side also. The fear of nature, which both men and women have, becomes unconscious, and spreads to include all women, the feminine, dreams, all "lower races" and "lower things." By 1750 or so the fear of nature had become unconscious. The old fear of nature, so natural to the Eskimo, and to most primitive people, attaches itself in a comfort civilization to invisible elements, which can never be defeated and never loved either.

Literature and art that attempt to reopen channels between human beings and nature, and to make our fear of her dark side conscious, help us to see her without fear, hatred, or distance:

> *There is a stillness*
> *On the tops of the hills.*
> *In the tree tops*
> *You feel*
> *Hardly a breath of air.*
> *The small birds fall silent in the trees.*
> *Simply wait: soon*
> *You too will be silent.*

A Meditation on a Poem by Yeats

THIS IS THE LAST essay in the book, and so I'll declare myself on a few points. I have not yet made up my mind how much consciousness there is in stones or plants, or what kind. And I have not said what I mean by "consciousness," as in the sentence, "There is a consciousness in trees." I have used it without defining it, because what we are talking of falls between all the words in English. What is inside a cottonwood grove or a hill is not exactly consciousness, nor psyche, nor intelligence, nor sentience. The psychic tone of nature strikes many people as having some melancholy in it. The tone of nature is related to what human beings call "grief," what Lucretius called "the tears of things," what in Japanese poetry is called *mono no aware*, the slender sadness. Buddhists associate the "slender sadness" with the incessant wheel of reproduction, going on without pause. James Hillman in *The Dream and the Underworld* suggests that the consciousness of nature is related to Hades.

I don't want to imply too great a unity in nature's consciousness. The varieties of consciousness inside things can be suggested by the way a ray of light unfolds into a certain abundance as it passes through a prism, from red, through yellow and green and blue to violet. One could say that the consciousness inside the badger belongs to the violet band, with much night-vision and melancholy. Trees belong elsewhere in the spectrum.

Sociological thinkers in the Descartes orbit sometimes describe consciousness as the ability to digest and process sense input, and produce from it points of view or concepts. Other people describe

286

consciousness as the ability to order. To me, the main quality of consciousness is that it gives off energy. The greater the consciousness, the more intense the energy it gives off; and it is possible that the more the consciousness moves over toward the red, the more perceptible the consciousness is. To become aware of the consciousness inside an object, we need to become aware of the underworld and the dream, and become aware of energy leaving an object and entering our body. So we become involved in the whole area of energy leaving and returning.

In this meditation I am going to suggest several different ways of talking about the interchange between the human being and the treetops, that is, nature. We start with the idea that it is possible for energy actually to leave the human body, though we cannot see it leave. It leaves, looking for ground.

The concept "electricity" and the visualization of the electric current is surely a great intellectual leap of the human being. Each invention in the outer world gives us a new vision of the psyche, and brooding on how electricity passes through wires or air, apparently "called" by a ground, we have for the first time a model for the way some psychic energy moves. Freud gave this energy the name "libido," and he and Jung wrote the first speculations about it. Instead of "libido," I'll call it here "desire-energy."

Plato returned again and again to the fact that human beings were drawn by tō kalos, "the good and the beautiful." That is strange. And Kant thought it the key to understanding perception. Why should "the beautiful" excite us to action, why not the ugly, or the wet, or the stormy or the passive? People will die for beauty; that is odd.

In this meditation, I'll ask what the concept of electricity contributes to this old question. When a person looks at something he or she considers beautiful, something happens; I'd like to try to distinguish between three separate things that are going on.

If I have the sensation that a woman is extremely beautiful, that is because my desire-energy has already gone out there, half a second or so before I "saw" her. My desire-energy, like all intense energy, is looking for a ground, and it will pass out through the eyes. The phrase "How beautiful!" is the sound given off by the desire-energy as it leaves.

Then it's possible a second thing is taking place. Her beauty, which is interior and complete, and not "in the eye of the beholder," calls out to an energy in me that loves beauty. Beauty itself acts as a ground. This calling is not sexual, and doesn't necessarily involve male and female. The energy I feel leaving my body could go to a beautiful teacher, to an old man, a young man, a well-made table, a shapely jar. Everything made in a shapely way implies consciousness; it even implies that the maker of the table is developing consciousness. If a woman calls out this energy, the movement itself implies developed consciousness in her. (The pin-up girl is a compromise; desire-energy leaves his body for only an instant, and then returns.) So this second happening involves more of the mysterious element of developed consciousness, won as the result of labor.

What then is the third happening? Inside me there is a woman, and to me she is beautiful. When I see a woman with a face somewhat like hers—I have never seen her—the woman inside me wakes up. So energy is passing between one beautiful woman and another. The fact that one woman is interior and the other exterior is confusing only to extroverts. And I am sure something similar happens with a woman when she sees a man she feels drawn to. As Dante says, "An intense man has the same effect upon a woman."

I'm suggesting then that desire-energy, when it is ready to leave the human body, can leave it, helped by the eyes, by three distinct paths, and the energy has been called out each time by a different form of "ground." There may be resistance or not . . . It doesn't matter . . . so much. In any case the desire-energy, penned up for so many hours inside the human body, has left, moving across air; and as it leaves, the person exclaims, whether he wants to or not, "How beautiful!" Sometimes only the first path is involved, sometimes the second, or only the third . . . or all three. Desire energy leaves through the eyes, but through other parts of the body also.

2

Keeping the three happenings in mind, we can try to see more clearly what happens when a human being looks at a grove of trees or a hillside or a waterfall. In a male, for example, the desire-energy moves toward a hillside as toward a woman the man finds beautiful. The hills are a ground themselves, and charged differently than our own bodies. The Greeks recorded strong sensations of sexual energy leaving their bodies, entering the hills or groves of trees, and returning. Stories of nymphs who are really trees, and the whole mythology of Pan and Dionysus relate to the first path. The desire-energy of both male and female experiences the hills or a waterfall as a ground. It feels them as a ground. The Chinese painting called "Li Po Looking at a Waterfall" broods on this mystery.

A second event is taking place as Li Po looks at a waterfall. Desire energy is as abundant as the water going over the falls. The waterfall is a model for the abundance and persistence of consciousness; the hillside with its apparent order is a model for the order of consciousness; a great stone shape suggests the highest peaks of consciousness in us. As the human being looks, he is struck by the immensity and variety of consciousness; he is drawn to it, and says for a second time, "How beautiful the waterfall is!"

We can, if we want to, recognize the presence of the third analogy too; namely, that inside the human being watching the waterfall there is an inner waterfall, an inner field of wheat with three crows over it, an inner grove of trees. What I am saying is this: inside the "human consciousness" there is a small bit of "tree consciousness." When that "tree consciousness" sees a large tree out there, it joins it, even over miles of air, and the man feels union with the tree. That is the experience called "The Garden of Eden," walking in the Garden of Eden, knowing that there is, in Wordsworth's phrasing, "something far more deeply interfused."

When there is a possibility of all three events taking place, then we can understand why a Chinese painter would be willing to spend a month painting a small scroll called "Li Po Looking at a Waterfall."

3

When the Industrial Revolution inflated the Westerner's view of his rationality, many Westerners apparently stopped exclaiming how beautiful mountains or waterfalls were. I've mentioned that travelers through the Alps during most of the eighteenth century don't report in their travel diaries much sensation of beauty. The Alps were experienced as a troublesome obstacle between France and Italy. Looked at historically, one could say that at some time in the Christian era, human desire-energy stopped flowing out into groves of trees and hillsides. The Church Fathers had always frowned on that flow, and in the seventeenth and eighteenth centuries the increasing ingenuity of Europeans in dominating nature lessened its value in our eyes. Finally the distancing formula phrased by Descartes declared that hillsides were beside the point in our new headlong flight into reason. The ego concluded that the countryside was dead.

Yeats wrote a marvelous poem, called "Fragments," which touches on this whole experience. Here is the poem:

I

Locke sank into a swoon;
The Garden died.
God took the spinning-jenny
Out of his side.

II

Where got I that truth?
Out of a medium's mouth,
Out of nothing it came,
Out of the forest loam,
Out of dark night where lay
The crowns of Nineveh.

Instead of saying that human sexual energy stopped flowing out into the trees and countryside once the Old Position had convinced people that it was dead, Yeats simply says, "The Garden died." We realize then that the Garden of Eden was alive only because men and women's sexual energy flowed out of the body and into it. At the time of Ovid, people still remembered when the route between the human body and the countryside was extraordinarily open, and this openness appears in story after story. In the *Aeneid*, Virgil breaks off a branch, and blood comes out, the branch speaks.

When Yeats says, "Locke fell into a swoon," he is summing up sixty years of experience during the Industrial Revolution, in which the inventiveness of human beings seemed a prophecy finally come true. William Irwin Thompson has meditated several times on the meaning of the Crystal Palace, completed in 1851; in this palace, for the first time in history, steel beams were used, with glass, to enclose living trees. That was a great triumph of the Old Position, because it said that human consciousness, now intensified and narrowed into "technology," had succeeded in its ancient war with the consciousness of nature, and won.

When the Garden dies, one doesn't have to bother with it. When the countryside is judged imprisoned, human desire-energy no longer goes toward it. As an analogy we could imagine the experience of a young man instructed on sexuality by an anti-female Catholic priest. The priest over several months gives the boy forty-two images of women's depravity, her uncleanness, lowness and wetness, so that when the young man sees her, nothing happens. His sexual energy stays inside his body, even when the sperm leaves. So when Descartes said, "I think, therefore I am," he meant the same as the Catholic priest: everything outside human reason is wet, vaginal, ugly, full of stupidity and night. Nature is a wet cave where death lives. The best thing that can be said for it is that at least it contains some space. The vagina and the womb have space, extensibility; deserts go on for miles; mountains rise for thousands of feet; stars have infinite spaces between; but that

291

doesn't change the fact that they are all disgusting. The starry sky and all its constellations are the cave where death lives.

> Locke sank into a swoon.
> The Garden died.
> God took the spinning-jenny
> Out of his side.

In other words, human consciousness decides to produce a dry womb. This womb will not be wet, males produce this womb, oh it is wonderful, it has a lining of bright dry stars, tiny linked fires go around the walls. Inside it is well lit with Edison's light bulb— the bulb itself is a male womb. Conception takes place without sexual contact, and when it gives birth, it is not through the vagina. No, light comes through the side . . . and what is born is the spinning-jenny that will pull men into factories, and away from the womb-like cottage with its dampness and its fireplace. We notice that the spinning-jenny is female, and the light bulb has a womb-like shape. That follows the Adam and Eve story—what is taken from the rib of man is female. When a man gives birth out of his side after Descartes, the new being is female, but mechanical this time. When a man is awake, he exchanges energy with the hills and gives birth to a woman, an interior woman. When a man is asleep, his energy remains circulating inside himself and he gives birth to a machine.

Once the spinning-jenny was born from the third rib of Descartes, or the fifth rib of Locke, it was likely that sexual energy would remain trapped inside the European body. Now desire-energy would no longer leap out of a human being, and suddenly appear as Dinonysus walking toward you with a soft hat, nor make a human cry come out of a tree. The human being was alone, Augustine had won; railroads are possible, vivisection is possible, a thousand muscular men with their sexual energy stored in their muscle system is possible, the Nuremberg rally is possible, doctors can begin their "war on death." After Locke's dizzy spell, men do not really subjugate a woman, they replace her with a dry womb, "a clean, well-lighted place," as Hemingway says.

To feel the contrast between our contemporary experience when we look at an object or a hillside, and the experience that is possible when an "opened" human being does that, we have to go far back into the past of the human race.

> Where got I that truth?
> Out of a medium's mouth,
> Out of nothing it came,
> Out of the forest loam,
> Out of dark night where lay
> The crowns of Nineveh.

Acknowledgments

Grateful acknowledgment is made to the following for permission to reprint copyrighted material:

Katerina Anghelaki-Rooke and Kimon Friar: "V" from *The Angelic Poems*, copyright ©1979 by Katerina Anghelaki-Rooke, translated by Kimon Friar.

Beacon Press: "The Simple Purification" and "The Clay Jug," by Kabir, English versions by Robert Bly. From *The Kabir Book*, copyright ©1971, 1977 by Robert Bly, copyright ©1977 by the Seventies Press.

Fred Berry: "Silica Carbonate Rock," copyright ©1979 by Fred Berry.

George Braziller, Inc.: "Stone," by Charles Simic. From *Dismantling the Silence*, copyright ©1971 by Charles Simic.

Michael Dennis Browne: "Lamb," copyright ©1979 by Michael Dennis Browne.

Copper Canyon Press: "On the Morning of the Third Night Above Nisqually," by W. M. Ransom. From *Finding True North*, copyright ©1974 by Copper Canyon Press. This poem also appears in *Carriers of the Dream Wheel* (Harper & Row, 1975).

Doubleday & Company, Inc.: "Her Longing," copyright ©1963 by Beatrice Roethke, Administratrix of the Estate of Theodore Roethke. From *The Collected Poems of Theodore Roethke*.

The Ecco Press: "All Hallows," from *The House on the Marshland*, copyright ©1975 by Louise Glück.

Farrar, Straus & Giroux, Inc.: "The Fish," by Elizabeth Bishop. From *The Complete Poems*, copyright ©1969 by Elizabeth Bishop.

Edward Field: "Magic Words," after Nalungiaq. From *Songs and Stories of the Netsilik Eskimos*, edited by Edward Field.

Geoffrey Gardner and Editions Gallimard: "The Call," by Jules Supervielle, translation copyright ©1976 by Geoffrey Gardner. This translation originally appeared in *American Poetry Review*.

Gregory Hall: "the voice of the power of this world," copyright ©1977 by Gregory L. Hall.

297

Index

MOON PIE PRESS